GW00689898

KID A MNESIA

KID A MNESIA

KID A MNESIA

THOM YORKE & STANLEY DONWOOD

CANONGATE

this book is dedicated to Radiohead
without whom none of this would have ever happened

the artwork in this book is by Stanley Donwood and Thom Yorke
with additional computer rendering by Nigel Godrich
and additional video work by Shynola and Chris Bran

acknowledgements from Gareth Evans:

for Stanley Schtinter
who knows
and in memory of Louis Benassi (1961–2020)
who remains the measure

all my thanks to Andrea and Tom;
gratitude to Andrew K. and Kamila K.

First published in Great Britain, the USA and Canada in 2021
by Canongate Books Ltd, 14 High Street, Edinburgh EH1 1TE

Distributed in the USA by Publishers Group West
and in Canada by Publishers Group Canada

canongate.co.uk

1

British Library Cataloguing-in-Publication Data
A catalogue record for this book is available on
request from the British Library

ISBN 978 1 83885 737 0

Design © Rafaela Romaya
Cover illustration © Stanley Donwood
Artwork from the albums 'Kid A' by Radiohead and 'Amnesiac' by Radiohead.
Licensed Courtesy of XL Recordings Ltd.

Printed and bound in Italy by LEGO SpA

After use remove Staples
Cut along Centre Fold
Place Pages in a Small Box
Place in a Drawer and Forget about.

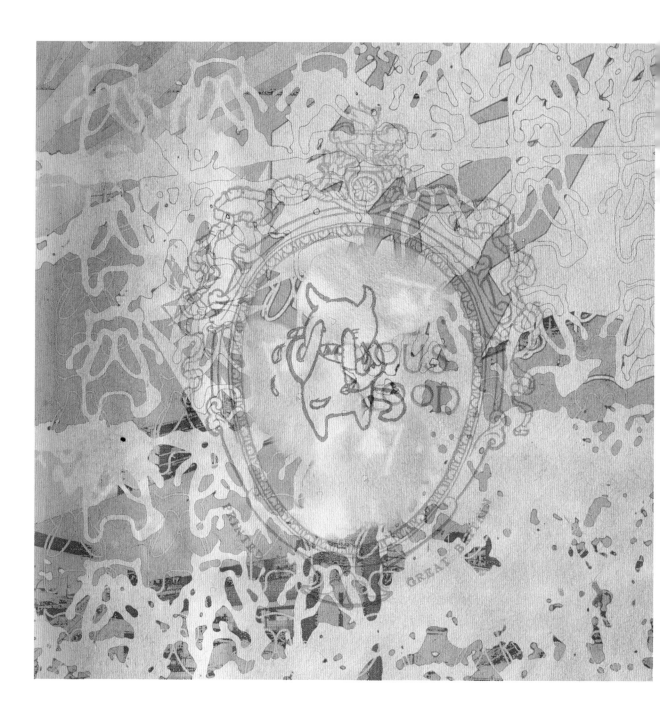

devils crying

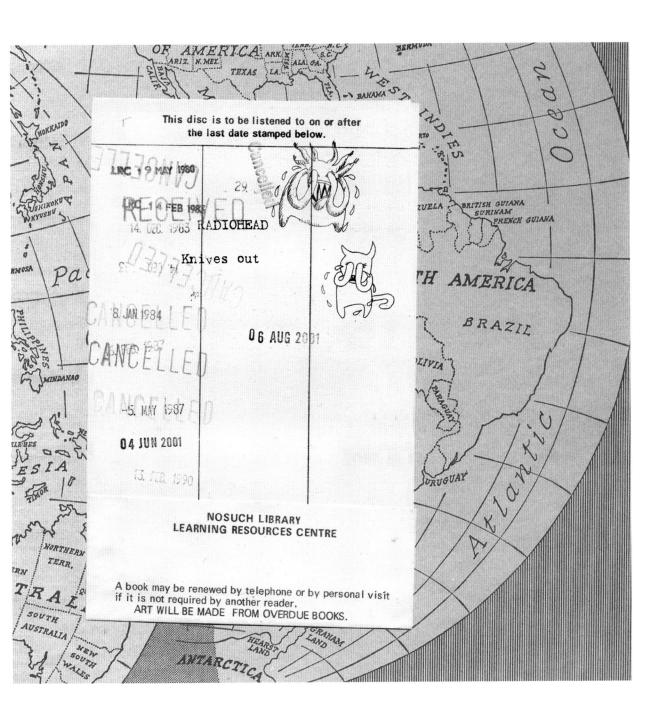

This disc is to be listened to on or after
the last date stamped below.

LRC 19 MAY 1980

RECEIVED
14. DEC. 1983 RADIOHEAD

Knives out

8. JAN 1984

CANCELLED

CANCELLED

-5. MAY 1987

04 JUN 2001

13. FEB. 1990

06 AUG 2001

INTRODUCTION

nothing to fear

STANLEY DONWOOD: Twenty years seem to have passed like nothing, but it really is a long time. I can't believe the innocent world we lived in when we were making this work. It was before 9/11, before the War on Terror, before the conjoining of the police and the military – all of the social changes that have led towards the position we now find ourselves in. I'm always trying to put things into context by removing a hundred years. So if we were making *KID A* and *Amnesiac* in 1899, 1900 and 1901, then we'd now be talking in 1921. The amount of time that has elapsed between then and now is huge. And the changes that have happened to society, culture and our understanding of history are also huge. It's very difficult to remember a time before instant news. It wasn't possible to know what was going on around the world in the same way that it is now, when news has become a sort of surrogate entertainment.

THOM YORKE: At that time we had this dream of a workshop space: an open space for lots of ideas. We were obsessed with the Can thing – we bought all this equipment, and set it all up. We wanted to be completely independent in every aspect of the production element of everything we were doing. And at the same time everybody involved felt like we'd been in some weird circus for quite a while, after *OK Computer*. Personally, I mentally completely crashed, as did Stan. We all did, in a way. Rather than immersing ourselves in this congratulatory atmosphere around us, we felt the total opposite. There was this fierce desire to be totally on the outside of everything that was going on, and a fierce anger, and suspicion. And that permeated everything. It was completely out of proportion, deeply unhealthy – but that's where we were at. So it was impossible to even start work, for a long time.

SD: There was a lot of jingoistic triumphalism in popular culture.

TY: We felt that there was a sort of uncomfortable shift in awareness going on. Maybe that was the fairly rapid disillusionment with Tony Blair: all the Cool Britannia nonsense, and all the artwork – the kind of thing that was called 'BritArt', and the YBA phenomenon that preceded that period . . . it just didn't speak to us. What we were listening to, what we were reading, was the total opposite of that. The phrase 'spin with a grin' was flying around at the time, because of the aggressive and self-serving PR tone coming out of the New Labour government. It was a strange new phenomenon to behold, and one now taken for granted: an obsession with how one looks rather than what one does.

SD: There was a lot of disappointment about integrity, or lack thereof, pertaining to Tony Blair. We'd made all this artwork that depicted fires, nuclear explosions over America and the Twin Towers, the World Trade Center . . . and then 9/11 happened and you had to go and promote the record in America.

TY: But why were we so obsessed, for example, with drawing the trees and all that sort of stuff? Part of it was that I had made the decision to sort of spend a lot of time in Cornwall, and Stan and I were travelling around a lot together in the landscape . . . and do you remember, the first place we went to, when we first started, was Paris? Because we wanted to build a studio, and it wasn't ready, so we went on this very strange trip to Paris, and we went to this exhibition—

SD: David Hockney in the Pompidou. Incredible. It was just basically loads of canvases, but felt like you were in something the size of the Grand Canyon. And that's what kicked the whole thing off: let's make these massive landscapes, these epic things.

TY: And then we were in Cornwall, all inspired by Hockney, wandering out onto the moors – do you remember this?

SD: It was freezing.

TY: Bitter cold. And we only had all the wrong colours, and these big canvases—

SD: I thought it would be really funny if we painted just in shades of blue and purple.

TY: We sat down in this stone circle, and we were painting for ages. And this old couple came and talked to us – 'Oh, what are you doing?' They were looking forward to looking at our paintings. And they were all fucking . . . blue and purple. And they walked off without saying anything.

SD: The next set of paintings we made were quite large – six feet square – and we started them in a freezing cold warehouse in Bath and finished them in a freezing cold barn in Oxfordshire.

TY: It coincided with the fact that I'd a had a complete creative block, and Rachel, my partner at the time, had said, 'Stop trying to make music. Stop completely for a while.' So I was wandering around just drawing anything I could see. Landscape. So landscape became an extremely important part of what was going on, because it loosened me up. When I did eventually start thinking about music and we started getting together again, landscape had freed me up, and I know Stan was into that stuff as well.

SD: Just creating a world in which you can tell a story. I felt like I was just full of stuff that I wanted to get out – all these ideas, all these interpretations of current affairs, politics, history. But it felt like you couldn't do it in isolation: you had to build some sort of structure that it would make sense in, otherwise you'd just be a loony on a bus.

TY: You can pick up either of our sketchbooks at the time and both the monologues are perpetually self-destructive. So the act of sitting down in front of a landscape and just trying to represent that in whatever way we felt – choosing to listen to that and not any of the shit in your head – was a massively freeing experience. I spent a lot of time alone, trying to get rid of this self-destructive noise in the head. Putting it in songs is a way to disempower it. You're working all the time, so you're not thinking about it. So things will pop out and you'll be like: 'I've no idea how that arrived.' That's always the case to some extent. But this one was like a tortuous journey from almost total gridlock – complete lack of confidence, complete cynicism in our own success, not feeling in any way connected culturally with what was going on in our own country, but at the same time being aware that we were in a really privileged position.

SD: We were *incredibly* aware of this *incredibly* privileged position that we were in. And at the same time I was sort of like consumed with a sort of a gnawing concern that . . .

TY: . . . it was all bollocks. Approaching every day as if we're total bluffers and someone's going to find us out at any moment.

SD: So, no change there.

TY: At that point I was fucking hard to work with musically, because I had a very fixed idea in my mind of what something was, and I would not shut up until it happened, which was very hard for the rest of the guys. But when we finally made it to our own studio, I had this choice to walk away, and go and play with Stan instead. It gave the others space, but it also inspired me in a different way.

SD: It felt as if you heard the music in a different way when you were up in the mezzanine as well, because you're a kind of observer then. You're not in the making space.

TY: Because it was the Radiohead studio, we were able to work on the artwork in the same way that the band were working on the music. We could just try loads of stuff. We had two studios and a mezzanine all running, and if something was down in one studio or it was a bit boring, you'd nip to the other one. There was a moment where – as far as I was concerned – we totally forgot about the idea that we were even making a record. To the point where I was going a little bit mad, because I constantly kept bringing new ideas all the time, most of which were shit. There was a point where everybody had to say to me, 'All right, look . . . we need to move on to the next bit.' But it was a long time before that happened – months and months.

SD: The music seemed to speak to me in a way that Radiohead's previous music hadn't done. It felt very *now*; it felt very *important* in some way. And so all I had to do was find a way of extracting what the music looked like from the music.

TY: There was no map. We just were trying to be very, very instinctive.

SD: It felt like – if a method was developing, that was a *bad* thing. If you're doing things by a method you just end up with the same result in different iterations. We were trying to destroy methods, to destroy habit. Basically, really perversely trying to make things as difficult as we could all the time.

TY: I don't think we needed to try. It's just what we do.

SD: The two records to me, in my head, felt very different. *Kid A* was these increasingly urgent answerphone messages left on a phone that no one ever listened to, and *Amnesiac* – I had this idea that *Amnesiac* was songs that had been left in a drawer in an old dusty chest of drawers that had been left in an attic. So both of them were kind of . . . kind of crying out for attention, but had been forgotten. I was spending a lot of time in London – I had this idea that if I filmed London, I could understand it. So I was going out and making these weird films that made no sense, and I was reading lots of books about London in an effort to understand it. Peter Ackroyd's book [*London: The Biography*]; Michael Moorcock's books about London [*Mother London, King of the City*]; Iain Sinclair [particularly *London Orbital*]; [Giovanni Battista] Piranesi's engravings of the imaginary prisons . . . I think I went a bit mad, because I did start to think that London was a kind of prison.

TY: I don't know why you started drawing minotaurs – I don't know why that started.

SD: The labyrinth.

TY: He was banging on about this all the time, the labyrinth thing.

SD: I was obsessed with it . . .

TY: On and on and on he went. And it really formed part of what was happening. The minotaur cursed to repeat its mistakes in a maze. We had this whole plan worked out for this ziggurat, where people could log on, and build a room in the ziggurat themselves, and leave messages for other people—

SD: And they had to use a certain number of characters. We basically invented Twitter before Twitter, and failed to make any money from it.

TY: It was called the Byzantine Ziggurat. But we didn't want anyone's data, therefore it was never going to work.

SD: I was a real evangelist for the internet in the beginning; I thought it was going to be amazing. I thought it was going to be like Gutenberg's moveable type; it was going to revolutionise the world, and it did, only in a way that I didn't foresee. A couple of years ago, there was a report about some guy who'd been on the run from the police in China. He'd been hiding from the police for two decades or more. And an unmanned drone, operated by a remote operator, saw some rubbish that he'd chucked out of his camp on a remote mountainside. They launched a manhunt, and they captured him, and they locked him up. For me, that's the internet now. There's just no escape. It's kind of the worst – it's become the worst thing that you could imagine.

TY: But going back to the artwork and the music, to me, the creatures in the *Amnesiac* artwork really felt like the abstracted, semi-comical, stupidly dark false voices that battled us as we tried to work. Personifications of the mood of the time, that flowed in and out of the songs and writing. The faceless terrorists; the self-serving politicians; corporate bigwigs hugging. It's there in *Fear Stalks the Land* as well: there are these people trapped, this character, this person trapped in this set of walls they built themselves, and they can't get out no matter what they do.

SD: We spent months or years or however long it was generating all this material, writing and pictures and ideas, and then just had to distil it down and distil it down into these two record sleeves, and that was leaving behind a lot of work. I think at the time, we thought that we were making the best of a bad lot. It felt like – for me, anyway – all of this was completely ephemeral. I had no desire to preserve it or archive it. Luckily Thom did. It was very much a means to an end, and it was a means to avoid having a method of working. We could just kind of splurge, and then focus on what was good from the splurge, so all of this stuff – now, twenty years later – I really like it. It's slightly like the diary scribblings of a couple of mad people, but it's also very . . . of the time.

TY: What we did in that period . . . that was the first time that I really felt this idea of synthesis, between being . . . well, I don't really consider myself an artist. I'm a musician who trained in art and then discovered that the two informed each other. But I always felt that it was a madly creative period, and I'd always wondered whether we'd missed something. I had always harboured a desire to reveal all the stuff that we'd kept in boxes around that period that didn't make it. The nature of being a songwriter, or a painter, or whatever, is to retain a beginner's mind. The search is the point. The flailing around is the point. *The process is the point.* I like being given material and maybe finding a narrative that someone else doesn't see. I like when Jonny gives me a piece of material, or Stan gives me a bit of writing, and I say, 'This bit, and this bit.' And then likewise that will get done to me. Stan is very good at being able to see something in something I did that I was literally about to bin. That means you're always working beyond what you expect.

SD: It's very easy to discard stuff that you on your own – as an individual – think was rubbish, but in fact it's really good. And at the same time you might not want to discard things that should be discarded. It's much more productive working with other people than it is working alone, I think.

TY: Yep. Always. The simple fact that we never even thought it was a problem to paint on each other's paintings, and write on each other's writing . . .

SD: We would start on two canvases next to each other, and after a certain amount of time, swap over and start working on the other one. And basically keep doing that until someone had . . . 'won' the painting.

TY: Always him.

SD: Yes, but I'm not very good at music, so it's fair. And with the writing as well – it was a very kind of like – back and forth. I tend towards a very over-meticulous, over-detailed, slightly anally retentive style of writing and drawing and painting as well. And Thom's sort of the opposite.

TY: Couldn't be more opposite.

SD: But this is the thing – that's what works. It's like a kind of kinetic energy that comes into something; that enlivens it. The paintings that we did in that method worked really well.

TY: I'd be going off on one in all directions, flailing around, experimenting with lots of different things, not even worrying whether it was going to be lyrics or not. And Stan was doing the same; Stan had also been writing short stories, and that was influencing me as well. It spiralled.

SD: *Kid A* has always been my favourite record, because it was so difficult. It was so hard; it was wrenched out. I'm more proud of it because it was so unlikely. When the record came out, I kept playing it and playing it – I was completely obsessed with it. I couldn't believe it had actually happened. A significant chunk of my life, distilled into two pieces of vinyl. It was amazing. So I hope that this iteration of it will speak in the same way. But we're probably just shouting into an endless vacuum.

TY: Fucking hell.

SD: Sorry . . .

TY: I would like to think that the freaky nature of how we went about doing all of this, for anybody that's interested – I hope it inspires a way of celebrating this idea of process. Just to let the boat drift and see where it's going to go. Don't jump out; just see where it goes. Not necessarily wanting end results; not necessarily trying to get to an end point. That's really important to me. Out of the First World War, and out of all the positivism of the Industrial Revolution, there was this disillusionment in the 1920s, right? You had this terrible Spanish flu, millions of people dying – and at some point it lifts. It all lifts, and then you get the Roaring Twenties. You get this *explosion* in music and art and film. What's really interesting is that we're witnessing on one side a determination by certain states, like Britain, to engage us in some horrific kind of doublethink. Being told how wonderful everything is when literally thousands of people are dying every day. Being told by the government how well they're doing. That's what we're ingesting. But we're also desperate for something real and true that speaks to us. People have been reading more. They've been watching films more. I feel that there's going to be a massive reaction. *Kid A* and *Amnesiac* are, if nothing else, a celebration of what is possible when a bunch of people get together and forget about everything except trying to create work that speaks to them at that moment, in a sort of frenzied, last-days-on-earth kind of way. I don't know why we thought it was the last days on earth, but I guess we did – it was the millennium, whatever. But that kind of madness is important.

That's certainly how I've seen it, digging through this stuff – going, 'Who are these people? They need help', but at the same time being really proud of that room of people doing it.

SD: That was great.

TY: What?

SD: You were being really articulate; it was fantastic. Fortunately, it's recorded; we can use it. We should listen to that kind of useful madness that we had. We didn't know what it was at the time, but it seems very prescient. It seems very appropriate.

TY: There's a weird thing about *Kid A* and *Amnesiac*. If you isolate lyrics or elements of the artwork, so much of it is indulging in this crazy sense of isolation and disintegration. But when we got to the end of the process, I felt the total opposite of that. I felt there was an underlying unity to what we'd done – a desire to express something beyond all the anxiety and excessiveness and self-destructive analytical bullshit. Maybe this is why the landscape thing was so important. In the end the music and the art that we made had a weird sort of holisticness to it.

SD: It's not a scrapbook; it's not a collection of singles – it's a complete entity, the music and the artwork and the blips and the way it was promoted, or not promoted. It was a very cohesive art project. Better than art school.

TY: We finally applied our training. The only thing I would have said to me then – to all of us, but especially me – is, that voice in your head that's telling you to torch the tapes and walk away, that everything you're doing is shit? You need to give that guy a firm talking to. You think he's helping you out, but he isn't.

SD: I can't believe I was such a fucking pessimist. Now that global warming has been sorted out and all conflict has been resolved, my gloomy take on existence seems ludicrous.

KID A MNESIA

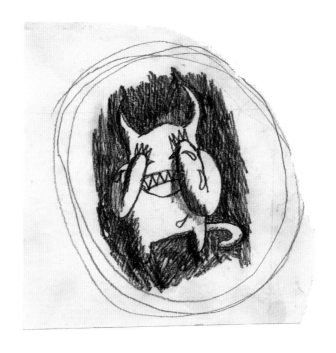

another minotaur

old tree

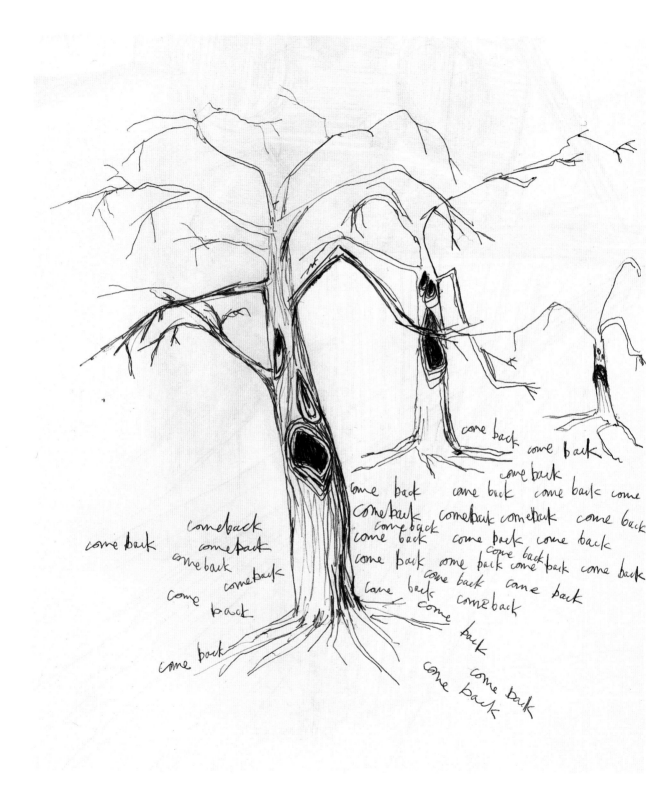

wood of suicides

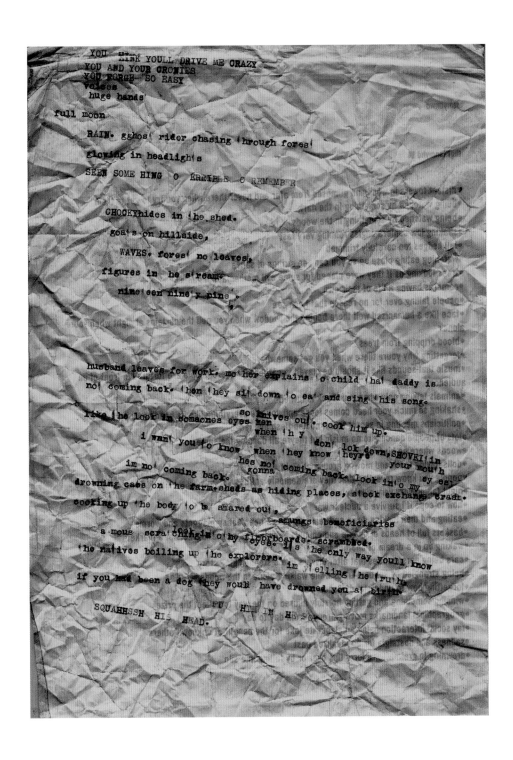

YOU THINK YOULL DRIVE ME CRAZY
YOU AND YOUR CRONIES
YOU FORGE SO EASY
voices
  huge hands

full moon

  RAIN. gghost rider chasing through forest

  glowing in headlights

SEEN SOMETHING TOO TERRIBLE TO REMEMBER

  CHOCKYhides in the shed.

   goats on hillside,

    WAVES. forest no leaves,

   figures in the stream.

     nineteen ninety nine .

husband leaves for work. mother explains to child that daddy is
not coming back. then they sit down to eat and sing this song.
                              so knives out. cook him up.
rip the look in someones eyes men
                             when they   dont look down, SHOVEL in
     i want you to know   when they know theyre   your mouth
       im not coming back.   hes not gonna coming back. look into my
                                                                    eyes. es
drowning cats on the farm.sheds as hiding places, stock exchange crash.
cooking up the body to be shared out,
                          amungst beneficiaries
   a mous scratchingin my floorboards. scrambled.
                                    eyes. its the only way youll know
the natives boiling up the explorers.
                                    im telling the truth
if you had been a dog they would have drowned you at birth

SQUARRSSH HIS HEAD.

cornish acid

wooden woods

cornish acid very odd

dream tree.
except it was

dream tree

dream tree / minos wall

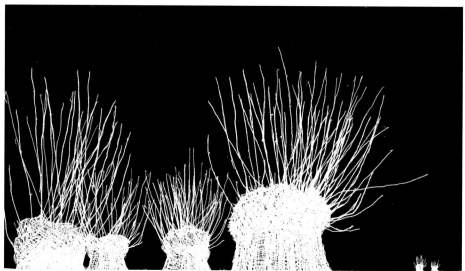

amoebae / amoebae2

im a machine to record the noise made by a plant wilting a mouse dying a hinge rusting a newspaper rotting a meal cooked left on the table uneaten drying carried away into the kitchen scraped into the trash the plate washed up the detergent bubbles dying leaving tiny traces too tiny to see on the china stacked back up for ANOTHER DAY.

like spinning plates.

Why did this have to happen now?
not changing time say
to
that this just feel.
like
spinning
plate

they'r killing all the tall thin ones
one slip and you'll be off
they'll feed you to the lions
your not allowed to make mistakes
cogs
Sa grey cogs
skirting round

i must keep my balance
i must be please the crowd.
don't give me none f you bullshit
no more
emotional
blackmail

While you score points and take pots lots
we all get cut to (shreds)
while we re begging to your cameras
you're making making pretty speeches.
and this must feel like spinning plates
our bodies floating down the muddy river.

a delicate balance.

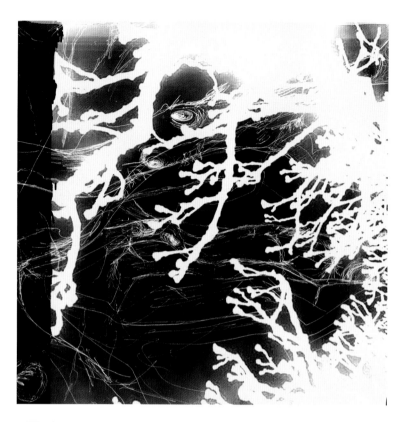

treefingers / minos wall5

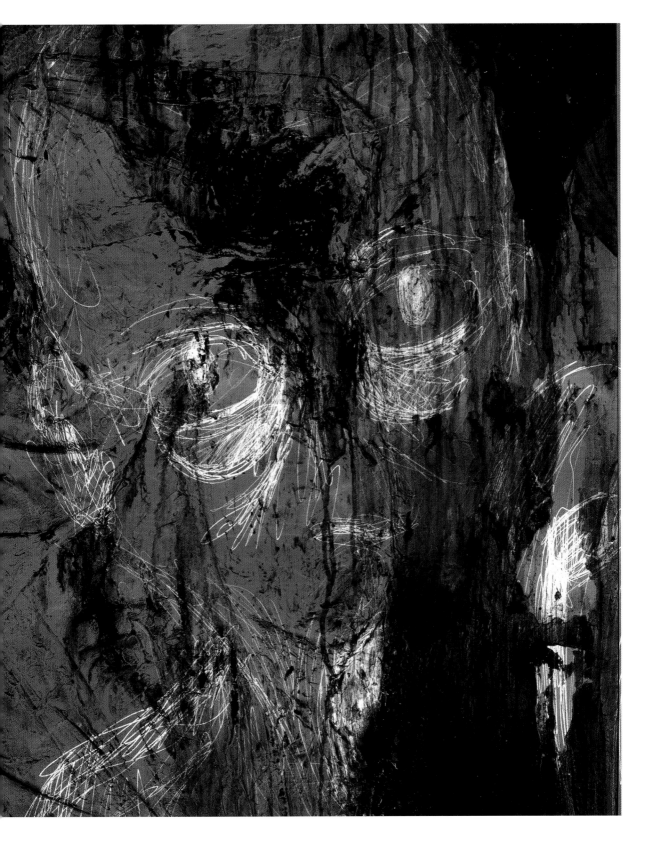

in need of comedy

minos wall I (detail)

minos wall I

minos wall II (detail)

news segment

good kicking

minos wall III

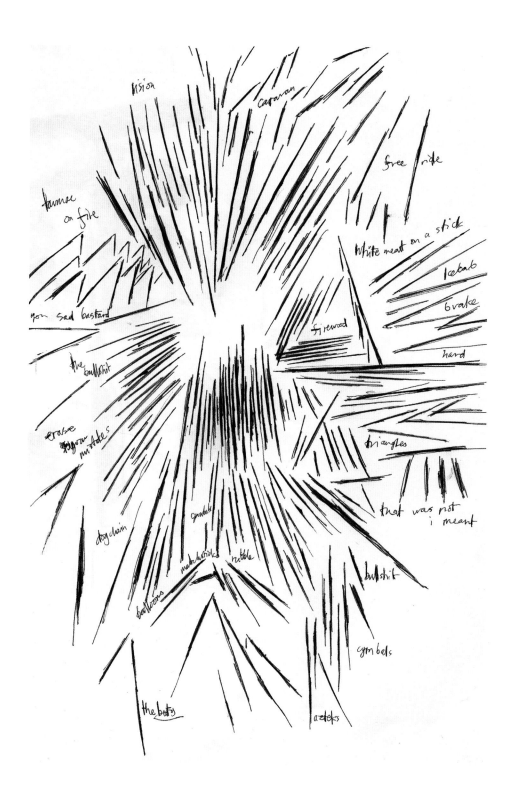

☐ I am bad. I am to blame.

☐ I think a little more sucking-up is needed.
☐ Food and water crisis developing.

☐ Words on a gravestone: I waited but you never came.

☐ What will we mean? Nothing.

☐ General loss of interest.

☐ He'll do something silly.

☐ Winning. The last player left in the game is the winner.

☐ A smile like the grim reaper.

☐ Children go to school tied together, led by parents.

☐ Airport closed. People coughing yellow phlegm.

☐ Not sleeping okay. Trapped in hyperspace.

end.

questionaire added2   { 27 }

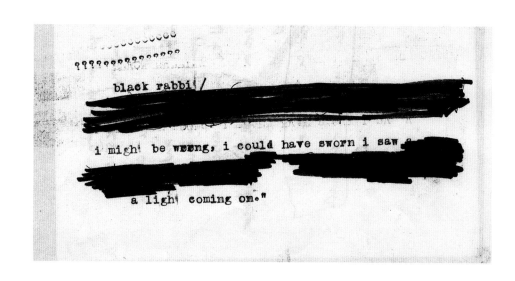

black rabbi

i might be wrong, i could have sworn i saw

a light coming on."

might be wrong

troubled forest

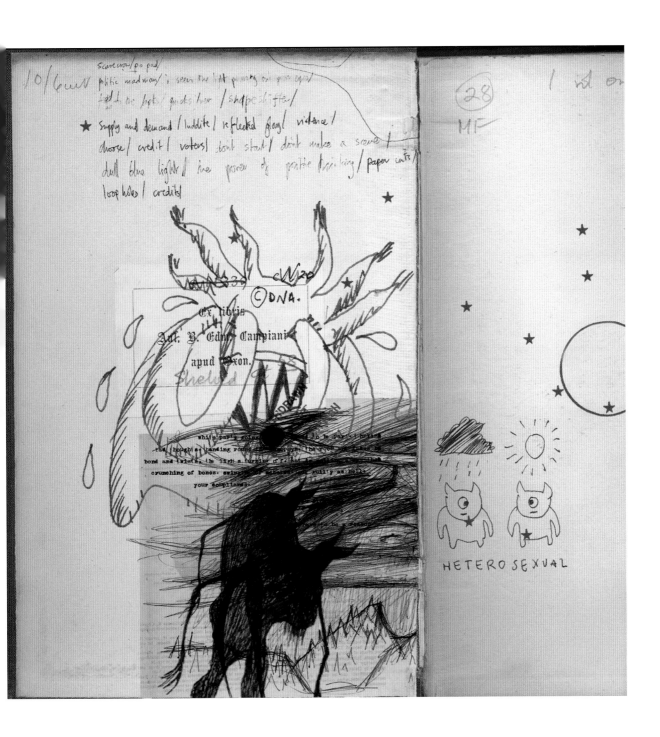

while party going ... to be part. baring
bad thoughts. handing round ... cropeye. the room and ... bend and twists. the lights turning off. set ... crunching of bones. swinging ... and guilty as hell.
your compliance.

things fall apart

husband leaves for work. mother explains to children that daddy is not coming back. then they sit down to eat and sing this song.

like the look in someones eyes when they know they're gonna

drowning cats on the farm. sheds as hiding places. stock exchange crash. cooking up be body to be shared out. savings. beneficiaries and scratching at the floorboards. scrubbed. the needles boiling up her explorers.

if you'd been a dog they would have drowned you at birth.

husband   {33}

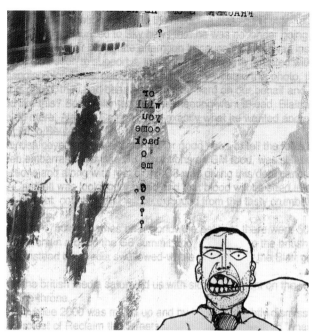

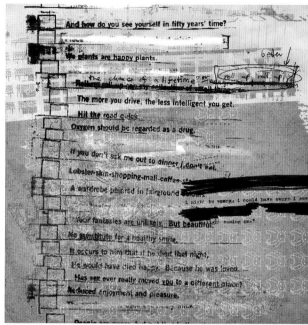

building drawing

testing oldpaper

furnace for the burning of money

prissy boxes

a ARK, complacence |. rivers rising. doors shut in yor face
whispering electronics, private security. underground bunker s
in London. rooms where you are forgotton. mental home. sectioned,
SEC IONED

SEctioned, sectioned. sectionedo sectioned o sectioned · sed ioner
sectiond sce ti osec ionecejb

sced ioned sce tioned secction

sce m ied sec tio sec tioned sectioned sectioned sectioend sectioned ser

sectioned sce tir r scetiom d sce tioned sec tioned sectioensectioend
sectioned sectiond sectioenscei tme sec tiond scetioe d sectioend

se sectious esec tiond sectiond section sectioned sectioned sectio

sectir iier

why did this have to happen now?
    not having time to say.
eyre killing all the tall thin ones. they feed me,
XXXXXXXXXXXXXXXXXXXXXXXXX XXXXXXXXXXXXXXXXXXXXXXXXX
u r bodies floating down the muddy river.

    (pulling wires from the ground)
    packt like sardines in a crushd tin box.
(XXstruggle.)

OOOH! MISTER BEAR! HELOOO!

    seagulls. swvsrm in the forest. so g memor
lokking down evaluating, judging, going to
or straight to hell. in wood of suicides. har
the branhches. souls begging for peace. stuck
wood. begging for respit to swish them well.
and for ourselves. the clouds daren and cough a

das boot

NO NO NO NO
crawling.

bones c... ...ing
supper. ... ...ir y w...
...ing fur. ben... ...t o me. ...ouldn
...rappe d in ... ...d in happier times. no...

... any ... ...in happier times. im ...
...b... ...ing ...round he table.
...

...reaking house. ...ing speaking.
...on hs. chaos.
...ove.

... monday.
hopeless case.
howling fon the chineychimney.
release me. release me, please. o please. please.

don... be so pathetic, stand up. dont let yerself be run down.
...hen game is lost,
GAME OVER;

lots of creatures

during glasshouse

mad bull

piranesi plinth

9.BUSINESS AS USUAL

(your name here)

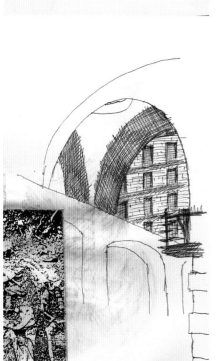

carcere04 / corridor / carcere07 / carcere06

buttress outline old

my attempt5 / forest prison

big fall

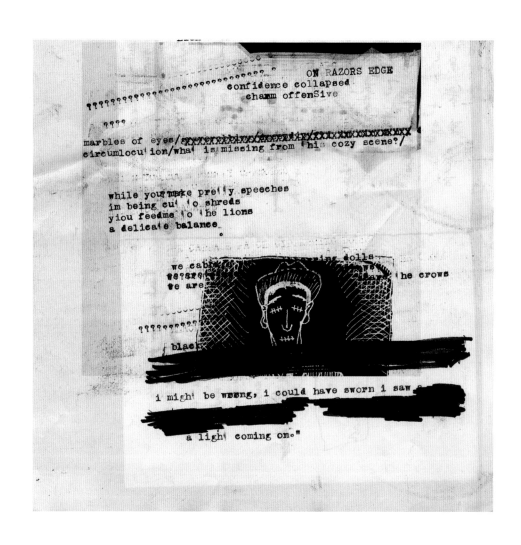

ON RAZORS EDGE
confidence collapsed
charm offenSive

marbles of eyes/xxxxxxxxxxxxxxxxxxxxxxxxxxxxxxxxxxxxxx
circumlocution/what is missing from his cozy scene?/

while you make pretty speeches
im being cut to shreds
yiou feedme to the lions
a delicate balance

we cab   ring dolls
we?are   he crows
te are

?????????

blac

i might be wrong, i could have sworn i saw

a light coming on."

delicate balance

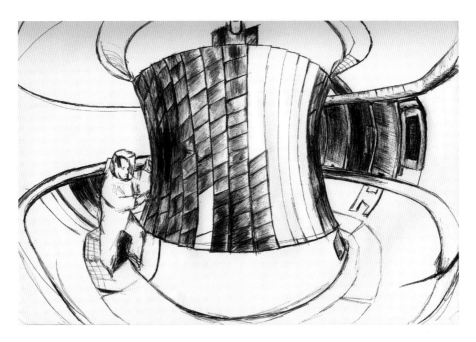

world trade old

will you come back to me?

you sunk my battleship / surveillance trees old
you sunk my battleship better / surveillance trees old2
surveillance trees / its groovy baby

after years of waiting   nothing came, as your life
before your eyes
  you realise, you realise,
  before your eyes, you realise,
              long fa air conditioning tubes,   archw
   rain,
   continuous rain,
   overhead cables humming
  snakepits,
OUBLIE Eprisoncells hebacksofpeoplesheads, grandmo
    andu

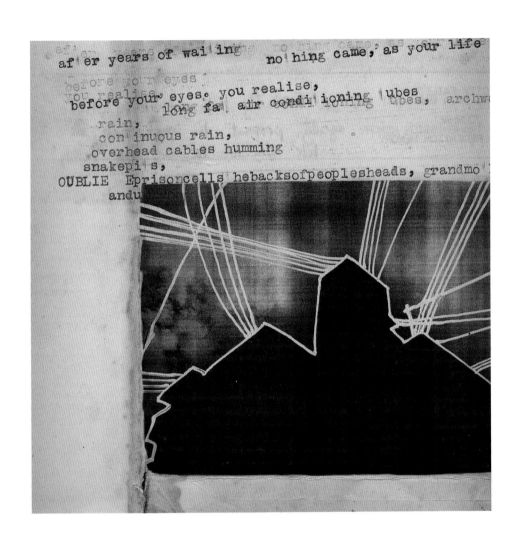

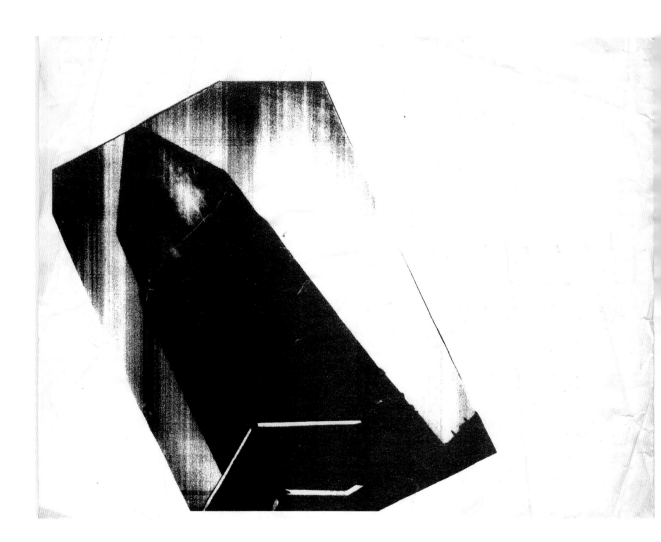

temple photocopy

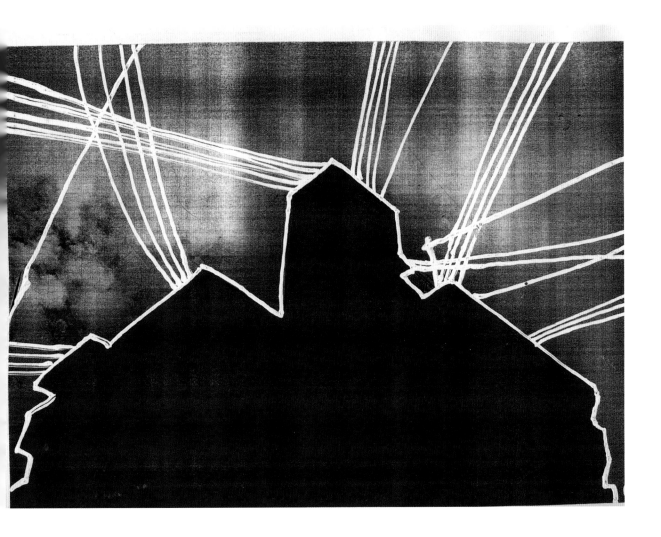

black castle wires

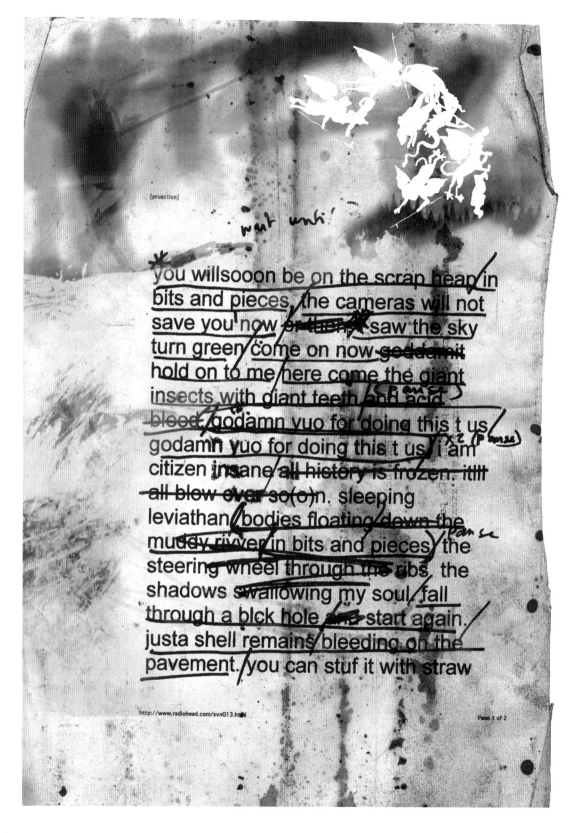

[proactive]

not until

*you willsooon be on the scrap heap in
bits and pieces, the cameras will not
save you now or then.* i *saw the sky
turn green come on now goddamit
hold on to me here come the giant
insects with giant teeth and acid
blood. godamn yuo for doing this t us.
godamn yuo for doing this t us.* i am
citizen insane *all history is frozen. itll
all blow over so(o)n. sleeping
leviathan bodies floating down the
muddy rivver in bits and pieces. the
steering wheel through the ribs. the
shadows swallowing my soul. fall
through a blck hole and start again.
justa shell remains bleeding on the
pavement. you can stuf it with straw*

citizen insane3

cloud cookoo land fig2

two towers

oldpaper3 idea

THERES NO SUCH THING AS SUCCESS.
I HAD SO MUCH TO SAY AND WHEN I FINALLY HAD A CHANCE
TO SAY IT I STOOD THERE SILENTLY LIKE A DUMB MOTHERFUCKER

Erethay isway onay uchsay ingthay asway uccesssay.
Iway adhay osay uchmay otay aysay,
andway Iway inallyfay adhay away ancechay otay aysay
itway Iway oodstay erethay ilentsay ikelay away umbday
otherfuckermay.

tokyo pyramid3

tokyo subway2

trees in subway

tokyo wires / wire minotaur / ziggurat

shamans tent

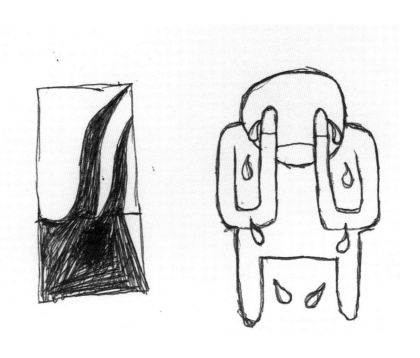

minos and a victim

photocopy city2 / maybe new york2

photocopy lines in rock

single tower

in the bunker like sitting ducks
for the exosets and scuds
do we look like the enemy to yu?
500points.
bonus round.

two towers 3

and money buys you anything at all
we can see you for what you are
we forgot why we started at all
these are bad clothes for rich people
uniforms for cocain discos
everbody has a price
your just fashionably left wing
and ythe shit that you cant dance to
this is music for rich people
were all commies and perverts here
we dont know whats happening.
as we await the backlash
this is music for stupid cash
this is music for rich people
we are not very scared of you

inner voice
pops and cracks
whooshes and splashs
laughs and then turns on its back
blows and then freaks me out
blows like a cave.

cocaine disko all you like / opposite: cocaine disco

old paper merger / merger

episode #38 probably   where we unveil the . . .

.. newtest-merged leviathan sea Monster. [off-shore]

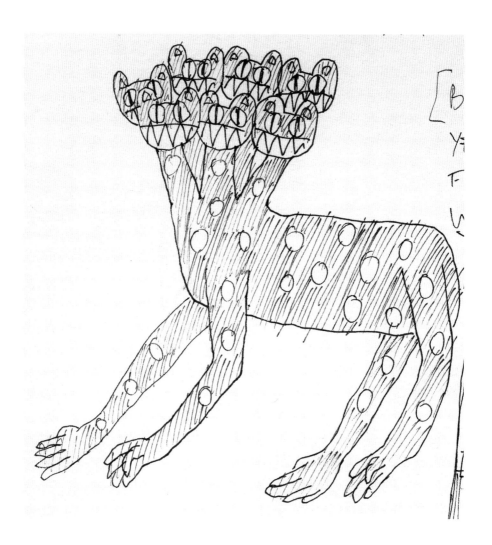

many headed beast

HUG NOW FUCK LATER

fuck later

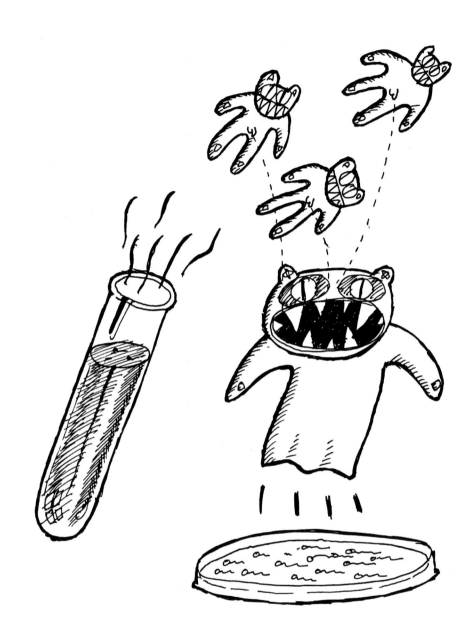

sperm ejac

bugsperm monster

you have three children right?

nervous?

collision better?

crimean war wounded3 detail

packed up like sardines in a crushd tin box

knives out

on the run with bears

desolate blue scene

googly minotaur

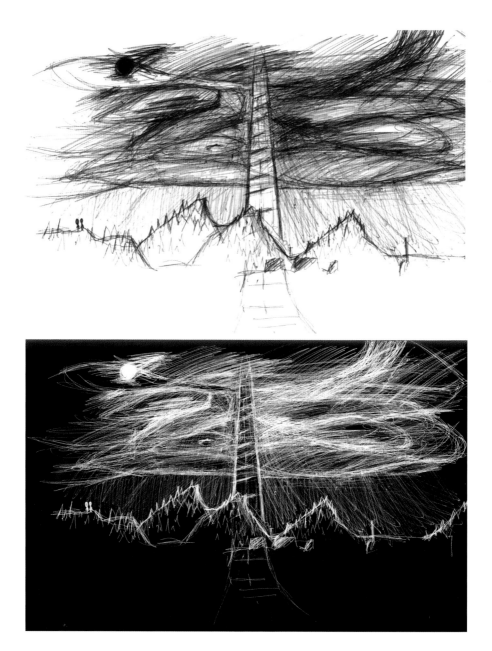

eclipsesmall / eclipse

red sea eclipse very red

modems squawking and splutterir
million gallons of piss on an infern

hissing like piss

Just a million mobiles and
d hissing like piss on a fire like a
st think of that eh? just think of that.

graphlands teepees

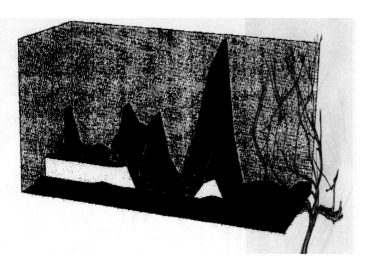

teeny tearful minotaur

bondjamesbond

wifey and hubbie choosey

the best cliffs contrasted more2

the master = race · superbeings - builders - slaves.

pyamid 2 study

j18 dalek invasion

unfinished landscape

thoms forest / bear forest

thoms j18 better

j18 dalek invasion with children

☐ I am bad. I am to blame,

☐ I think a little more sucking-up is needed.

☐ Food and water crisis developing.

■ Words on a gravestone: I waited but you never came.

☐ What will we mean? Nothing.

☐ General loss of interest.

☐ He'll do something silly.

☐ Winning. The last player left in the game is the winner.

☐ A smile like the grim reaper.

☐ Children go to school tied together, led by parents.

☐ Airport closed. People coughing yellow phlegm.

☐ Not sleeping okay. Trapped in hyperspace.

end.

i cheated (what detail?)

residential nemesis (detail)

hotels and a swimming pool

get out before saturday (detail)

get out before saturday (detail)

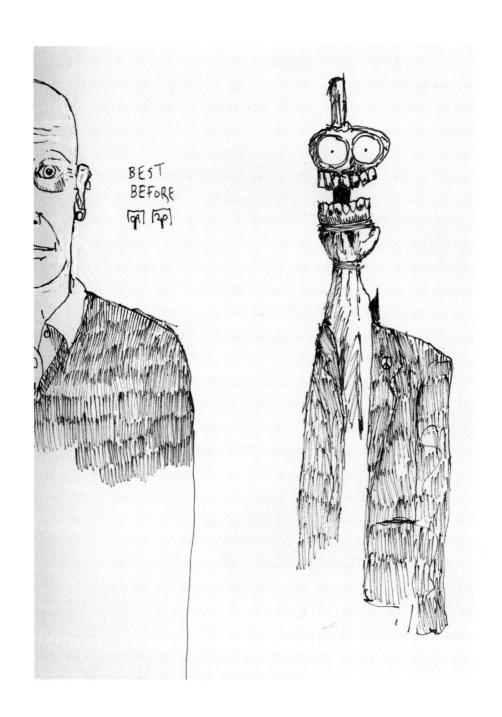

BEST
BEFORE

scarecrows

ME
ENTO
MEI
2000

SCARE THE CROWS, PIXEL A momento of ME

happy scarecrows brown

a nice straight road with nothing coming

blair-love   photo opportunities

walk on casualities   wife swapping

standing in the shadows at the end of
the bed

traffic bad   unsatisfactory

leave all that stuff alone
it s over and done with now

RADIOHEAD

UNDER A BIG TOP
TRICKLEDOWN COMPRESSOR
UNSURPASSED NOVELTIES
GIANT COGS TURN
WELL ADJUSTED
THE ICE AGE IS COMING
RUBBER BULLETS
LAST REMAINING
POLAR BEARS

A GENUINE
FREAKSHOW
150,000 VOLTS OF ELECTRICITY!
MOBILES CHIRPING
CRACKS APPEARING BENEATH THE VENEER
ABBATOIR NOISES
WEAK RECEPTION
OUR NAME IS LEGION
CARROTS & STICKS

PACKT UP LIKE SARDINES IN A CRUSH TIN BOX

SHELLSHOCK, PARALYSIS, SLEEP-
WALKING, any Child who is Backward
in Study, and BAD HABITS of any
kind PERMANENTLY REMOVED, Etc.

For a Due appreciation of the above
INCOMPREHENSIBLE MUSICAL COMBINATION,
much and a little more is depending on
the Imagination of the Audience.

FEAR STALKS THE LAND!
I AM AWAKE AT 4AM TO THE TERRIFYING UNDENIABLE TRUTH THAT THERE IS NOTHING I CAN DO TO STOP THE MONSTER
POSTER BY TCHOCK & STANLEY

tent tour poster

KID ALPHABET
A Mortal Beings Index

BY GARETH EVANS

Apology

From Late Latin, Greek: defence, justification

Words fail. These words. These words fail in the face of the evidence, the project: sonically, virtually and visually. Socially, too – impact assessments, registers of reach, amplifications / redirections of technology, innovations based on trust: strongly agree, on a scale of one to, add your comment here . . .

You have already heard from Stanley Donwood and Thom Yorke. Their lines might wonder and wander but they don't flail – they issue from *inside* the operation. These, however, *stumble*; they veer, doubt, come in slant. They are not *about*; they draw *from*. They speculate, associate, recall, reconsider, reflect; they don't try (how could they try?) to explain. How could they, and least of all to you, dear reader-viewer-listener-participant-*fellow traveller*, you who surely knows more, far more, than this correspondent about the material under inspection? You might have grown up / alongside / into this work, been nurtured into sentient, comprehending personhood by it, had the veils drawn from your perception by it, the doors of experience swung open and through you went . . .

So please find these entries only as stand-alone but communicating way-markers, station stops on a single respondent's journey across the terrain. There are countless approaches that can be made, have been or will be undertaken, but this accumulation is offered as a kind of 'running alongside' Radiohead as they stepped across their alchemical threshold; trying to keep up for sure, moving forward while looking back (pillar-of-salt time maybe, but we're only human, more or less, after all . . .).

It's placed in the order we've come to expect from language, but please don't look for a linear passage (no narrative arcs here). The energising exemplars in this regard are 1) B.S. Johnson's *The Unfortunates* (RIP): a box book, 27 separate sections and, first / last apart, able to be read in any order (15.5 septillion possible combinations, it is noted); and 2) Julio Cortázar's *Hopscotch* (*Rayuela*, 1963), with a variety of progressions proposed for its 155 chapters. 15.5 septillion? How can we take that on *even as an idea?* And 1963: you've got to be kidding; the year of JFK, when the straight line of history was shot in the head in Dallas.

You see what I mean? It's starting already, the forking paths . . . hypertexts *avant la lettre*, they speak from sites we might wish to call prescient. So this A–Z is offered in a similar fashion. Certain 'go to' options are suggested, but these are indicated precisely so that they can more easily be ignored. Compiled in the spirit of rumour, whisper, early-hours compulsive association, mad-eyed guesswork, hearsay, paraphrase, it might suggest voices in the street partially caught as they climb the airs and stairs of evening towards a midnight balcony. Call to mind the overheard, the glimpsed, books mis-shelved, reels mis-labelled, emails mis-sent, the torn cutting, the found photograph, the unposted letter, the dusty chatroom thread still growing like empty mansion ivy in some far corner of the network . . . music from down the hall, mutterings and the shadow of boots in the bar of light under the door . . .

Perhaps it's really about atmospheric disturbance, pressures in the public realm – their making and their reception. Pattern recognition. Tracking the times as they manifest in the works made; works that then go on to manifest the times.

It's about the place you've been on the fold in the map, the co-ordinates you wrote down on a ticket or the back of your hand, the swathes of 'general impression', or where the charts give up entirely. Never get out of the boat . . . unless you are going all the way . . . *This* doesn't go that far, but it could be argued they did then – and do (a crew of seven in a workspace under the name Radiohead, the Radiohead Seven), and so at least this text knows the direction of travel. Essay, from the French *essayer* – to try; Beckett tried, failed, and so on, better than we could ever hope to, and in the Gallic too. Let's bring it closer to home, as Shepperton's finest, J.G. Ballard, writing right under the flight path, noted, 'deep assignments run . . .' – you'll find it if you need it. I'm sorry.

Before

the sea, the standing stones, the turning constellations . . .

You are in a room – it is very late or very early or both – in this way you have the run of the clock – each wall has a window – every compass point is open to you – there is floor wall to wall for now but the roofing is uncertain – beyond the room you hear the sound – it is growing and it is the sound of a growing sound – what a sound sounds like as it becomes one – it is a sound which makes pictures in your eyes and it is a sound that makes a space in which you can be something you are not without it – you very much want to be part of that sound but you are not sure from which place from which hour it is coming to you – so you wait – you stare intently at your hand – at the labyrinth of your fingerprints – you feel the path to the sound is within you and without at the same time – it is the same path but it looks different in each place – it is bright and dark threatening and exhilarating – so you wait – at the edge of the times and the turn of relations – while everything you know everything about your life and place everything inside your head and not is just about to change . . .

Alice

From Old French, Old High German: of noble kind

Open the file on *Kid A*: the one they can't name, the victim, the charged, the one with their face pixelled out, the one with their words but not their own voice, the one we last saw on CCTV, the one who rabbit-holed off. Follow the thread and try to keep up, the crumbs in the wood, the labyrinth red. Reorder the search space to fit with the need: Depth-first then Bruteforce. Go figure, go, figure; figure it out. Peel your eyes, skin your ears, Treefingers primed: in the country of the virtual, the one with touch is king (of limbs and so much else). You're a witness at least, maybe more. Where were you on the X, and with whom on the Y, and what were you doing on Z?

I remember *Memento* played out across screens twelve days after the record's release. Mind how you go: in a land without maps pay attention to signs. Don't forget to remember, something at least; why not the Motion Picture Soundtrack? Don't outsource it all. The Citadel knows far more than it should. But does it know this? A kid is a gathering of atoms for peace.

See also –
Amnesia (anteretrograde)
Ariadne's thread (logic)

Assistance –
Amnesiascope (Erickson, Steve)
I Remember (Brainard, Joe)
Je Me Souviens (Perec, Georges)

A
——
148

Aleph

From the Semitic: ox

The Aleph is an open door on blueprint plans for building. Please note the fire exits and be alert to trip hazards. It is the bull, corralled, systemic animal; the 'monster' in the machine that wants out as much as Ariadne does. In Borges' story of the sign, there's a domestic Buenos Aires cellar on Avenida Juan de Garay. In it, on a step, rests the Aleph, a panoptic marble of cosmic dimensions. It delivers total vision (the writer's protagonist is not the only subterranean; later, much later, for those who attend, they shall be gifted in rainbows live from the basement).

But that's not the sole Aleph. Word is that there's a stone pillar in Cairo's Amr Mosque that, while it can't be seen, emits a dynamic hum suggesting universal action to those who practise patience in the wait (we shall not linger long with another very different Aleph, although this company does promise 'a suite of data analysis tools for investigators' and we shall certainly accelerate beyond legal limits past this final financial Aleph, which claims to 'think differently' and who 'back companies driven by secular industry themes'). Dollars and Cents; so it goes . . .

The codes in language are pictures of the possible given sonic shape and purpose. Taste intention on the tongue. Let the throat conspire with breath to make something that was not there before. There is a trembling, sonic tremor on the wall of Plato's lung. The body knows its calling to be sound.

A

149

See also –

Aah / Aargh / Abecedarium / ADSR / Aerial / Affect / Aghast / AI / Alarm / Albion / Alert / Alienation / Allegiance / Alpine / Ambience / Amplification / Analogue / Android / Anger / Animosity / Antenna / Anxiety / (Ant)Arctic / Ardour / Art / Attention / Automation

Auxiliary –
The Botanical Mind (Buenfeld, Gina & Clark, Martin)
Sign and Design (Kallir, Alfred)
Wild (Griffiths, Jay)

Body

From Old English: trunk of a man or beast, material existence of a human; related to Old High German, but otherwise unknown, and no longer in German or Germanic; for the OED it is 'a great and important word'

We are sacks carrying the organs of ourselves. The foundational fact is this: Joseph Heller knew. This is the true Catch-22. The body was and is there. It tells us what we cannot bear to know, whether we like it or not, while the mind, given the facts (wrench, spasm, ache) either denies or endorses, as is its wont.

So we cannot remove the body from this assessment. It's hard to know How to Disappear Completely when you're obliged to drag one of these around. Absence can be the most vigorous form of presence. Sometimes, to vanish is to appear, and fully. Hard, though, harder than ever . . .

And yet new species of body are emerging, and fresh ways of being in them that are closer to becoming than to the perception of simple entropy: each reflex an action, each reaction a proposal. The first body in question here is Thom Yorke's; primary, or so it appears, the bounded one that holds 'Thom Yorke' (TY), but where he ends and we begin is unclear. We are aware that our resource footprint – which allows us to be who we are – presses hard on the face of the globe entire, while our creative, emotional, intellectual, social incarnations extend far beyond the kilos and bones. We do not stop at our body's shore but travel on without feet across the wide ocean boulevard of all that is other-else-not us / us at the same time.

Multiple selves – named and not, as we all are – he 'embodies' but his public 'self' is the activating factor. His bodily motion suggests far more of process than of what we take in ourselves to be a stable flesh. As his lyrics indicate, this character is both assailed by external forces but also resistant to, and challenging of them; marionette and puller of strings. The judder, the time-lapse shudder presents a kind of erratic, evading target, a constant sloughing off of imposed skins, of fixed definitions, boundaries and frontiers.

Such mobility operates by definition in the present of its enacting but has now accumulated such an archive that he has to a certain degree freed himself of time, shaken it off, and not only in the way that any photograph or film does, at once of the split second and catapulted clear of it. Rather, his sometime ecstatic progress – an entranced and entrancing secular pilgrimage towards fuller incarnation of the push / pull impulses of being alive – is something encountered, 'owned', remembered, re-presented, told and transmitted far beyond his ability to contain. Truly he has become the multiplicity.

This can involve a *Twin Peaks* style of red room rewind and reversal, a masque as much as it is TY wearing the mask called 'Thom Yorke'. Performance is the body declaring itself vigorously to exist, and most widespread in this case, just as language is not really a virus from outer space but an emission from inner space, the body's material tools attempting to help the mind seem reasonable – or not.

What charges this so provocatively is the acute visual delirium of Donwood (SD), whose artwork across all his deployed media features innumerable figures who echo and amplify TY's variant positions and perspectives. Isolated, at risk in vast territories of hued distress, in calamity and crisis among the hostile towers of cities, or singular on elemental slabs, they are at once us and we wish they were anyone else but us. *That couldn't be me; let it happen to someone else . . .* Their forms look like they are already their own chalk outlines, dead people walking, shades and barely shaded simultaneously. Even when they're shunted into crowds, it feels as if it's only a matter of time before they're rumbled and the threat will find them out, one by one, once more. The secondary twist lies in the sense that even the overtly aggressive individuals feel similarly as vulnerable as the innocent. Given the vistas they're at work in, this is hardly surprising perhaps, but it strengthens the pictures, plummets them beneath the painted / scrawled / inked surface into caves of contradiction.

Bookshelf –
How to Disappear in America (Reid, Barry)
Vanishing Point: How to Disappear in America Without a Trace (Bürner, Susanne)
Vanishing Point: How to Disappear in China Without a Trace (Bürner, Susanne)

B
151

Countryside

'Any tract of land having a natural unity'; country, from Old French, Vulgar Latin: land lying against, opposite or spread; side, from many: flank, long part; music on one side of a phonograph record, from 1936

Can they return to the 'land' to find their new groove? Yes, they can. Open all the gates of the rented estate and begin to traffic in transformative energies. Place is the place: the Cotswolds this time round – the novel, radical edge, both origin and departure point. Jurassic limestone, it goes all the way back. Escarpment and valley, open, wooded and pasture; it is the English offer manifest. And being thus, it also has in its gift a range of US and national air force bases, a Cold War bunker or two, a landscape militarised and fit for purpose: fabled 'unsinkable aircraft carrier', forward base for American nuclear payloads. Add in pliable local officials all too ready to bend to prevailing power and this island has it all when it comes to geopolitical manoeuvres.

So place – with its stored, stacked arsenals, its ability to render ghosts as the knacker does his horses – is tension in three dimensions. Fear stalks it. Beneath the foot it rumbles, in the air as the wind in the wires or the upper floors of the mansion, the Marie Celeste rooms (creak of the timbers, the banging door), in the scare birds on field racks, in the head at 4 a.m., some lost month, bearings shot. Tune into it – no choice – it's found your dial and the station can't be changed. You can't hold it, like the music (not the artefact, the vessel, the carrying device, the merch), you just listen and it's off, on its journey to the stars.

Saint Jerome in his study – everything there, from his skull (not his, the one on the desk, little bone cave) to his scripts – world within world – while the actual one (so-called) through the windows, vaguely seen, persisted: something like that, it was, yes, as we recalled. Making the place fit for the making of sounds not heard before. In retreat from the polis all the better to see it whole, the core of the corruptions, the damaged bigger picture; remove oneself to drive forwards, among the failing histories of the fields; as the high houses, adrift from the age, unanchored to the viable reality of things, sink among the grasses and are gone.

Consider –
Patience (After Sebald) (Gee, Grant)
Penda's Fen (directed by Clarke, Alan; written by Rudkin, David)
Underland (Macfarlane, Robert)

DeLillo

'I don't want to talk about it.'

How he speaks to us, in American, about all of our times: their artesian wells of twisted faith and magic, their paranoid meteorology, their proliferating insanities, and their obsessive systems. Find the 2005 interview with French magazine *Panic*. There's his creed as a writer in a line or two: oppose, resist all structures, try and stand 'outside' (if that location even still exists). Don DeLillo published his first story, 'The River Jordan', aged twenty-four, in the Cornell University literary magazine *Epoch* (10:2, Winter 1960; he was a Communication Arts student at Fordham in the Bronx).

And here's something, shall we call it a synchronicity? His 1997 *Underworld* – the career colossus, a century summation, the pan-social epic, the deep dive – appears five months after *OK Computer* lands . . . the stunned responses, the exhaustion and the turning away.

So we arrive in the new millennium and with 2001, his next and slimmest, strangest book, *The Body Artist* (I don't need to join the dots), is published four months before *Amnesiac* is heard. It's a book of skewed memories, performance art, haunted houses, occupation, inhabitation, and a small man who looks like 'a kid' (the audiobook is read by Laurie Anderson, which will give you the flavour; 'No Surprises' there perhaps, which is the song TY dedicated to her and Lou Reed from the stage in their town, on the road in those febrile years between releases). Drop further down the wormhole and you'll find the music blog The War Against Silence (furia.com, initiated way back in the earliest epoch of its medium) and the 20 September 2001 post, 'Three Days in the Air' ('I am in seat 20A, looking out over the trailing edge of the left wing . . .') that tells you what happens when you go camping for a few days and hike right past history. It also hymns three albums: *Amnesiac*, Laurie A's *Life on a String* and Björk's *Vespertine*. Enough already, or never enough . . .

Which is to say that the 'Underworld' – closer to the mycorrhizal networks of fungi joining trees beneath the earth – is really a way of being in the world; a transport of ideas and associations, of desires, that links events and their report, people and their admirers, everything, as much as it generates a speculative glue between defining works. It is a place as much as an attitude and that place is called the Internet. But hold that thought.

*From his business card when living in Athens, 1979 (see Don DeLillo's America, online 3 February 1996)

Directory –
Don DeLillo: Word, Image, Gun (Evans, Kim)

D
___

153

Ecology

From Greek: study of a dwelling place

How is it that we haven't stopped hunting bears? We've known about this stuff for so long now. The world has been watching itself implode and they (SD, TY) were watching Worldwatch watch it all unfold. The Institute brought it to light – storm light – and, well, the lighthouse invites the storm, it seems. Denial spreads like blood on the swimming-pool tiles. Ice floes like our tears should (where pack ice should remain). There's been a calving: greater London has broken off Antarctica (Brunt Ice Shelf). This is not a seasonal breeding programme. The new drone is the ancient groan of such shelves collapsing into southern seas. This is not a drill.

This is the age of erasures, of things going for good (not good). Do you remember the house that drifted complete out across the ocean? Who lost the instructions for putting out conflagrations before they start? The scorched-earth earth is tired of all the blows. God gave Noah the rainbow sign: not only water but also the fire next time . . .

Human words about what to do feel increasingly like one of DeLillo's 'airborne toxic events': bomb, leak, virus, hate speech, fake news, lies. The 'atmosphere' in every sense has always been central. Stress fractures are found and felt in things that can't be grasped. Anthropocene, Capitalocene, Necrocene: whatever the scene, it's not pretty. There's a reason why SD is saturating the land with images of the blasted scape; just as with the figures, in an age of image overload, once you start to look, you cannot help but see. There is distress in the content and the medium. Foreground and background stain into each other. There is no escape from 'the problem' in either direction. This is less like 'taking a line for a walk' than dragging it to an atrocity exhibition.

The damage is both visible and not; what's inside, past unaided person perception, working its way deeper into the very fabric of matter. Think global, act local; fine and good, but why stop there? Think cosmic, act atomic, surely (although we're tossed on the devil's blivet, damned whichever prong we're on; our actions towards improvement making most things worse through previously unknown consequence – this is the nature of the tipping point and the feedback loop).

In the accelerationist present, ruins increase exponentially, but right now they are natural and not built. We need to climb the steps to an ecology of mind. Or else, the world we've made will end the made world.

E
____
154

Examples –
Finding the Mother Tree (Simard, Suzanne)
In a Dark Time (edited by Humphrey, Nicholas & Lifton, Robert Jay)
The Sensing Body in the Visual Arts (Driscoll, Rosalyn)

Friend/ship

From Old English: attached by personal regard and preference

The collective that plays together, stays together. Play is key – new toys or back to basics, children splashing in the puddles, making booted sounds. Wayward nights and days that stretch in real time, underpinned by tenderness: without you, I'm nothing.

Meeting people used to be easy. You would just meet them. Now we're ghosts in the machine and we haunt each other's platforms, feeds, for reasons more than viral in their starting. Where is the fungal thread of true connection, the arboreal understanding, the refreshed but enduring companionship of the Pando Aspen Tree Colony? 'Things lasting' is the new radicalism in an age of planned obsolescence and speculative demolition. This is not just a fridge-magnet mantra; it is where the important work is done, because it expresses its ethics through the example of the making, and not only in the declarations of the outcome. This extends to the crew, support personnel, backroom operations. Where corporations pillage, where cronies hollow out the assets of the state, so in the alternative networks of solidarity (which extend to interaction with the fans) we find the consolations of companionship. There is a continuing reward in this, a solace. Kindness comes from kin (family or not), in kind. It's not about life or art, but art inside life: taken together, the matter of being and thriving alive more than simply existing. Sail on.

F

155

Follow up –
Here for Life (Zimmerman, Andrea Luka & Jackson, Adrian)
The Mushroom at the End of the World (Tsing, Anna)
Social Poetics (Nowak, Mark)

Gesamtkunstwerk

From Middle High German: whole, entire work of art

Beginner's mind is open field and it stays that way. It understands the creativity that comes from balancing form and not-form, shaping emptiness. In that space meaning forms.

Remember the green fuse. Patience and flexibility; don't explain; don't make things happen but let them happen. Set things in motion. That is the task. Ask questions. Let others answer them. Once anxiety lifts, and the idea of both efficacy – and efficiency – is abandoned, then possibility emerges as a path. Intention is not the goal here. If you know what you are looking for, you might find it, and the journey is done. Without that, the voyage-quest-odyssey, all is just a formal exercise.

In all media, each distinct and reinforcing of the whole, vision stirs as murmuration and settles on the piers of resolution. Canyon and cliff, ruptured and reasoned, distressed and decided, the topography shaped is not a world wishing population, or a world view wishing conversion in its wake, but rather a glitch manifesto, a declaration of shards, a kintsugi conversation, and all the more resilient for that. Order and chaos are not opposites; both are positions in flux. Find your own location in that shift and, in time, you might just find a New Thing Breathing next to you.

Gift aid –
Afterlives of Abandoned Work (Harle, Matthew)
And Our Faces, My Heart, Brief as Photos (Berger, John)
The Gift (Hyde, Lewis)

G

156

Head

From Old English: top of the body, upper end of a slope

Wake precisely with the Morning Bell and stride out for the head/lands, to where the breeze is bright. Yes, a storm is tiding in – you see it from the cliffs – but draw a line beneath it from your tensed self to the ground and that will keep you somehow on the earth. The storm is history – see the angel in it, how its wings are beating, oh, they beat. Times are, there are times the mind slides on its own fast-cracking ice. I'm not here, or there, ideally I'm not anywhere – did you say that, on the ending edge, coated in the wind. Mind is all there is sometimes; it does your head in, because it's in your head. Days like this, you're out and all of everything is there. On others, it's like a tight, dark cave, oh, so deep, how far in, how little light there is, it does not reach. Music is interior life pressing on the air.

There's no way any person could convince a single other of this world's exist-ence, unless they wanted to believe.

What changes if we say a Radiohead, *the* Radiohead?

Find the work you want to make: first in the mind then find it in the work.

How about –
The Blind Owl (Hedayat, Sadegh)
Gravity and Grace (Weil, Simone)
Markings (Hammarskjöld, Dag)

H
—
157

Internet
Internet.com

Ask it what it is (ask the www).

Survey Report 10: from the rabbit hole, the black hole, the whole . . .

The Internet is –

1) short story 'Report on an Unidentified Space Station' by J.G. Ballard (1982, always ahead)

2) installation *The Coral Reef* by Mike Nelson (January 2000)

3) book *House of Leaves* by Mark Z. Danielewski (March 2000)

4) the Aleph

SD reckoned there was something in it. He'd spent a lot of time in digital cafés, wired in all the senses, had been a wrangling convergence pioneer. He was in demand on the circuit. It had all got a bit much. But he told the others and they were in. The official machinery hadn't noticed and it left them to it. Early adopters get the wormholes.

How innocent it all seemed (let's say it was, for now). We all think that but can we remember it, how it felt? Can we remember anything any more? Hope flowed through it like water into droughted fields; free from threat, finance, co-option, and commodification. Google was just half a house back then. Process was all: product was only manifest as part of that. Connection meant connection: the fans gathered and so the camp/sites spread, horizontally (read the comments; it so matters). And you shall know them by the trail of likes. You could breathe the trust in like an Alpine morning; not for profit but for play, not for gain but the game. Would it have made a difference if we didn't speak of going viral but of weeds? If it had been described in gardening terms and not the biomedical? Would it have kept us closer to the world? Now, like tarnished tree rings the Internet surrounds itself, swallows itself, and outgrows itself, an Idioteque. Something is taking its course.

Stay on the line, caller: your call is important to us. Dial out, dial in, dial H-I-S-T-O-R-Y. She* called it the 'portal' and, indeed, that's closer to the sensorium of it, the magical thinking, the crossing place, aperture in the real that can feel more real than the real. Don't reduce it to the technical, which is just the means, while we are told to dream of the ends, which we can never reach.

In the mix –
Dial H-I-S-T-O-R-Y (Grimonprez, Johan)
How I Became One of the Invisible (Rattray, David)
No One Is Talking About This (*Lockwood, Patricia)

(In)Justice

From Old French, Latin: quality of being fair and just, moral soundness and conformity to truth

Blessed the Fool
Who Speaks Truth to the King
And Yet Still Walks Away
With Their Life . . .

In recent years Facadism has been growing across architectural practice. The listed exterior surface, normally the street or public-facing aspect, is retained while the rest is demolished and rebuilt. Often the new build doesn't attach directly to the surviving dimensions but stands – or hides – behind it. Regularly, windows in each don't match up. There is a profound misalignment between the two. You can see where this is going.

What is said and what is done are not the same when it comes to corporate / hierarchical / institutional / state behaviours. These structures have always done this. Now it is the default position, and any small alignment comes as the shock.

Something happened.
What happened?
Something.
Was it bad?
Yes, yes it was.
Whose fault was it?
Not ours.
Not yours?
No.
Whose then?
Somebody else's!
Do you know whose?
Not yet.
But you will know?
Yes, yes we will.
And what will you do when you find out?
What shall we do?
What will you do?
We shall . . . we shall . . .
a) say that we're going to punish them b) ignore it c) encourage them to do more of it (tick all that apply) d) overcome . . .

Invisible forces rule our lives – yes – emotions and gravity, and others. Get an Amazon Echo for £0 when you join Vitality. The National Anthem can be applied to any occasion.

My SUV has been clamped. My basement extension has collapsed. My nanny has been deported. My housekeeper only works twelve hours a day but is still demanding the 'living wage'. Today's challenges require tomorrow's solutions.

I met a man on the open road. He was from a land to the east. His mouth told me of his cares. It said I am so broke. And mine said no the system is but you are one of its pieces. There is no single target. Perhaps there never has been. How do you target the liquid modern? The human body is majority water but is not a privileged part of this fluidity. That runs like floodwater or squirrels of flame up into the eaves. It is wireless, ungraspable. It lies less in the organising intelligence than in the capacity of that ideology to project. Not self or society but spectrum: full-spectrum dominance. Think of their images-texts-lyrics-records as documents of a distinctive defiance.*

Document: *from Old French and (Medieval) Latin: lesson, written evidence, example, proof; to show, teach, cause to know . . . make to appear right*

Defiance: *from Old French and (Vulgar) Latin: challenge, defy, provoke; renounce (one's faith)*

In Madison Square Garden he threw his voice like a dark bouquet out across the throng:

Bring down the Government . . .

Shut your hole!
Back in line!
This is your last warning!
Get out of the road!
I said, back in line!

*I am grateful for the insights running throughout Mark Greif's essay 'Radiohead, or the Philosophy of Pop' (n+1, 3, Fall 2005), reprinted in *Against Everything: On Dishonest Times* (Pantheon & Verso, 2016). Any misinterpretations are this author's own.

Jostling for position –
The Master's Tools Will Never Dismantle the Master's House (Lorde, Audre)
This Brilliant Darkness: A Book of Strangers (Sharlet, Jeff)
What I Heard About Iraq (Weinberger, Eliot)

J

160

Kafka

From Czech German: jackdaw

The kernel of this piece and his own clearest commentary: who could enhance his inexhaustible texts, certain of them literally without end or close, and so they are the emblems of this argument, in both form and theme. What we could perhaps attend to is the parable 'Before the Law' (you'll find it in *The Trial* and, since then, also out on its own) and to the fact that, in bed, in the days before his death (3 June 1924) he was editing his story 'The Hunger Artist' (at this point he himself could no longer eat).

As for his naming, let us only note, in association, that the gods punished Princess Arne Sithonis – she had allowed herself to be bribed with gold by King Minos of Crete – by turning her into the noted bird.

Keep –
The Lost Writings (Kafka, Franz: edited and translated by Hoffmann, Michael)

K
‾

Labyrinth

From Latin and the (pre)-Greek: large building with intricate passages; (palace of the) double-edged axe; narrow quarter; figuratively, bewildering arguments

Or how we all stayed home. But home is not a granted refuge (just as Life in a Glass-house offers a very ambiguous opportunity). Don't you remember the Lynchian corridors, their dry-as-a-throat darkness? Home can be an enormous space, one that grows in threat the smaller it is. What's that you say, how about you retreat into your own head? Forget it, we've worked that one through already.

Sudden jolts of lightning reveal the scale of the city, and the city is everywhere or else is not, and where it is not, there is nothing you can do to make that place a living. This is not about choice. The city is sheer. Its towers do what they claim. They are glass and steel, affording no purchase. Winds howl between them.

Don't follow me, I'm lost.

A labyrinth is not a maze but the words are all as tangled as the trail and both are patience card games (solitaire). For SD, London was a labyrinth, a multicursal, branching trap, a snare for agitated minds too ready to make links. This is not the single path of lifelong meditation. A few mouse clicks away from freedom, then, and the open air? In that version, you follow the thread to get lost, not go clear. You'd have more luck tracking your own red vein. So, pity the poor Minotaur, just as SD does. He didn't choose it either; to be born or to be trapped. Once you've been inside too long – him, sad bull, or us – things can start to blur. What was it Pogo once said? We have met the enemy, and the enemy is us. First we 'created the conditions' and, by doing so, step by turning step, we trapped ourselves within. Hall of mirrors? Sure, your face here and here and here: beast, walls and snivelling wretch. No single reading, single meaning is there to be found, however far you walk.

Do you remember the way out?

Way out? I didn't even know that I was in.

Listing –
The Angel of History (Forché, Carolyn)
The Maze Maker (Ayrton, Michael)
The Minotaur (Watts, George Frederic)

Möbius (Strip)

A non-orientable 2D surface with only one side when embedded in 3D Euclidean space

Midway on our journey we find ourselves in a dark wood, the straight path having been lost. All turns on the decisions we make now. Standing here, with each and every sound, however small, apparent to our ears, and searching for the faintest glow of field light through the trees, we can at least pause a moment to reflect on how we reached this point, this turning hinge, on which so much depends. In Limbo? Not quite yet. A simple twist in the trail and we are thrown back on our earlier progress. How can it be, and yet, and yet, it is. Such is the elegance, the beauty of the pattern here before us now. Could there be a clearer analogy for the recordings under consideration?

We know their shared gestation, appreciate their difference, understand their separation, bring them to attention now, two decades down the road, because they were the twist, and the gesture's startling new formation. So the binaries dissolve, a unity revealed, but one more complex, so much more, than any 'single' thing. Into this pour all your seeming oppositions, and find that they are never that: art / sound, individual / collective, motivation / result, process / product, transmission / reception, affect / effect, then / now, both / and . . .

Maybe –
Fever Dream (Schweblin, Samanta)
A Field Guide to Getting Lost (Solnit, Rebecca)
The Duino Elegies (Rilke, Rainer Maria)

M

No

From Middle English: not in any degree, not at all, not ever; from Proto Germanic: not + vital force, life, long life, eternity

A friend now dead found a dump of 16mm films in a skip on a London street: brigade shoots of major fires from across the century gone (west to east, Crystal Palace to the docks). It turned out they'd operate a three-ladder set-up. Two would carry hoses, the third a camera, rolling. They'd shoot the blaze; teach them better how to damp it down next time round. Then they'd film that one.

Earlier in this commissioning there was some concern voiced about 'mission creep'. The remit was generously wide open but the issue was with meaning, that it might find its way into the analysis. It was felt that the long leap, the joining up of phases was perhaps not useful, given how discrete and of its moment (brief or longer) each round of making was.

That's not to say there was a wish to build a gated community, 'secure by design', around intention, to stop it impressing itself on wider consciousness. It wasn't so much 'move along, nothing to mean here' as the perhaps understandable worry about claiming something; it felt more rewarding to stop making sense rather than to beget more.

The lyrics work to this effect, of course, each line a trip wire against neat progression. The spoken plea is met by violation, words work at odds to sound, the vocal pitch to what it proposes. There is the offer of a hand and then its sharp withdrawal. The language of blunt authority is deadened down by sound bites, startled by tenderness. Incantations, calls to rise run out of steam, are interrupted or ignored.

But the mind makes meaning whether it's there or not. It draws on the reserves of its own experience to find connecting tissue, to make synaptic leaps. Context helps this on, but meaning spills in from elsewhere, slips in between, or round about, at the edge, off the page, in the air untenanted by song. The same manoeuvres are at play within our viewing of the image bank. Despite the violent contraries there, the eyes scroll their sight across the plains; they want to understand.

It is in the common status of the soul to seek a place within which it can dwell. Feelings and ideas – material – pressed into form by intense application (neither content nor 'content' but uneasy and evasive of reductive description) work on the receiver in ways that cannot be prescribed, governed, even expected. This starts with a choosing to look at or look away. Tuning into a word, which might be a rent in the fabric between what appears to be and what is, the ear too pursues its comprehensive course.

Words and appearances can be deceiving. How do we 'read' the blossom in Pripyat? It is too much, isn't it? It's too charged, it's too 'blossomed'. It's exactly in this space – between the sheer exuberance and what made it so – that meaning is made: what this work does too, so vividly and rigorously. It recognises, but it does not remedy (who can?).

How many steps does it take – a letter at a time – to change nuclear to nothing?
Undo / Edit History / Clear History . . . but don't forget to Confirm Humanity . . .

Noted –
Coming Over Here/Nothing (Lee, Stewart)
greyisgood.eu (Callanan, Martin John)
To Those Born After (Brecht, Bertolt)

N
—
165

Oubliette

From the French: show negligence, forget; secret dungeon for prisoners without hope of release, a cruel and perverse punishment

'Packt Like Sardines in a Crushd Tin Box' is one way to phrase it, but this is something far less tangible; this is primal fear. Sometime back before *The Bends*, a man in Cambridge died. His lodgings, in a house surrounded on three sides by major roads, were found – when he was discovered by the stench – to be covered, ceiling and walls, with newspapers, pages and cuttings, on every solitary surface. He was both imprisoned and forgotten by the times themselves. They killed and then they buried him.

This, however, is a memory project; or more accurately, a re-membering. It is about reassembling the scattered body of the works, the generative momentum and their times. It's Godrich nesting up SD and TY's flock of flying faxes, logging that they'll be relevant 'later'. It's SD getting every image he made out of his head and off the walls, the drives, stacked in the drawers. And it's not that any of them need the digressive telling here: they're all so articulate (in mind and limbs, they're kings of insight into their own procedurals) and they seem to have recalled pretty much everything necessary.

But sometimes we must be able to forget, and not remain condemned, like Borges' Funes the Memorious, to recall everything, *every thing*. Nobody wants to be forsaken but what might it mean when one's dead wife appears, re-generated by memories intervened on, as happens to cosmonaut Kelvin in Andrei Tarkovsky's *Solaris*? (SD has documented Tokyo much like the Russian did, as a proposal for the future, for a future memory.)

It is said now that nothing is forgotten, and every trace remains, somewhere out there in the cosmopolis of ones and zeros. The political realm, however, feels like a deepening oubliette.

I keep forgetting how to live.

Operational –
The Fire Next Time (Baldwin, James)
In the Wake (Sharpe, Christina)
The Last Angel of History (Akomfrah, John)

Pynchon

From the Norman (Pontchardon) via Devon

Study for a portrait of Thomas Pynchon as a load-bearing wall: from where your correspondent is standing, in his sense of coded response, themes, range, attitude, stylistic virtuosity and productive adjacency, Pynchon is that important to this whole enterprise. To committed supporters, W.A.S.T.E. will not have escaped your attention. This moniker-sharing (for their social network) honours the covert organisation at large in *The Crying of Lot 49*, Pynchon's shortest novel but one of world-bestriding reach, influence and allusive, conspiratorial density, all of which might well have informed the band that less, durationally, is more when the less you have is packed with so, so much more than that of those who declare that they have more.

Pynchon is the epitome of the connecting (search and you shall find) engine. It all joins up even when it doesn't. This is all that can be said on the matter; otherwise we're done for. What we can suggest is that his most recent novel *Bleeding Edge* (17 September 2013), whose title could be one of Radiohead's, speaks directly to these albums' recording period and sensibilities, while his novel *V* (and even *Vineland*, let alone *Gravity's Rainbow*'s V2) calls for alphabetical interrogation (from the Egyptian through the Semitic and on).

The echoes of *V* (song to song) continue in 'We Suck Young Blood' from *Hail to the Thief* but that's a story for another day, along with Jonny G's scoring of Paul Thomas Anderson's adaptation of *Inherent Vice*; and, oh yes, did we mention the instrumental 'Thomas Pynchon', from MiniDisc number 3 (OKNOTOK) . . . ok, hold it right there.

Let's bring in some intellectual heft now, just to draw a line on vagrant speculation, by calling up Dr Abeer Abdel Raouf Fahim, social influencer and currently Assistant Professor in English at Abu Dhabi Polytechnic, whose doctoral thesis 'Redeeming the Betrayed Body: Technology and Embodiment in the Fiction of Thomas Pynchon and Don DeLillo' (Durham, 2012) might well be apposite here . . .

It goes where it must and it starts where it does. Pynchon published his first story, 'The Small Rain', aged twenty-one, in the magazine *Cornell Writer* (6:2, March 1959; he was a student at Cornell, studying Engineering Physics then English). He published his second story, 'Mortality and Mercy in Vienna', still aged twenty-one, in the Cornell University literary magazine *Epoch* (9:4, Spring 1959). His relatives got off the boat in 1630, and he has gone all the way.

Possibly –
A journey into the mind of < p. > (Dubini, Donatello & Dubini, Fosco)

Quest/ion

From Old French, Medieval Latin: philosophical or theological problem, a difficulty, a doubt . . . a seeking

There are five leading frames in which experience can be held and interrogated: the interior, the social, the architectural, ecological and inter-planetary. A migraine with aura is not the same as the aura around objects. A rainbow of oil in a pool sends out complex messages. Distress can be beautifully expressed.

Walking is leaning forward into arms that are not there, into a shelf of air. It is falling into its own momentum. Morphic resonance understands there are points on the dial that cannot be seen or heard. Life finds out life by all and any means necessary.

Be that infant, away into the park while nobody was looking, who asks later WHY and then why and why and why – all the WAY back until why becomes how. The further you question, the more your soon-to-be former being unspools like 8 mm stock from your wrist / chest / forehead / mouth (delete as appropriate) and you follow it as it becomes the tail that wags your future.

Attack, decay, sustain and release. Generate the envelope and then push it.

Query –
Border (Kassabova, Kapka)
Can't Get You Out of My Head (Curtis, Adam)
The Gold Machine (Sinclair, Iain)

Q

168

Radio

From Latin: beam; instrument for the production of sound by radiant energy

The paranoid impulse in 1970s and early '80s US cinema lay as much in the corruptions of the sonic as in abuses of the textual or visual. Listen in to *The Conversation*; decode the recording in *Blow Out*. As the greed decade developed, so did the tech: *Videodrome*'s rogue transmissions, dished out from a location all too close to home, felt like prophecy. The new flesh was found on a different kind of tape. By the 2000s, of course, it was wireless once again, but broad- not narrowcast. *Demonlover*'s dungeons could be visited between – or during – homework assignments.

Scan the frequencies for futures. Turn potential into form. If you could see the Babel of the air (as SD seeks to do), its googolplex speaking in tongues – witness *all the signals*, much as Ted Hughes' Iron Woman can hear the screams of pollution across the toxic marsh (the plants are monitoring us too), then you'd be bleached to bone in seconds. It's not just about volume overload – cochleal and retinal collapse – but also about that intention again. What to *do* with all the stimuli? You can't ignore them or dump them: they're not drying up any time soon. Like the Voyager golden discs, like every sound ever made, they're off on a very long journey – heading for a mash-up with the music of spheres – and there'll be new ones here before they've even left (might we have made first contact now if we'd sent *these* records out . . .). Think of TY as an aerial, an antenna in this tumult, and we turn to Turner's legend, as the artist, roped to the mast in the storm, paints it *from the inside out*. The weather is working on a self-portrait.

Receive and Transmit. There's a tension in attention, but it's not so binary; it's much more like 'Pulk / Pull Revolving Doors': which is it? Please decide. Afraid not, it's not that simple. It never is. You have to come at it oblique, oblique, oblique; you have to sound the sound for its depth charge. In the labyrinth of the inner ear, modulated in amplitude and frequency, you realise that dissonance is not the opposite of resonance.

Relevant –
Nothing in My Pockets (Anderson, Laurie)
The Origin of Others (Morrison, Toni)
Remake the World (Taylor, Astra)

R

169

Studio

From study v. & n., Old French, Latin: devote oneself to, show zeal for; state of deep thought or contemplation, mental perplexity, doubt, anxiety, amazement or wonder

It's helpful here that studio and album serve both the musical and the visual. Find SD on the mezzanine level of the barn, at it constantly with whatever came to hand: Knives, sticks . . . (there's a fine lineage here – poet Yannis Ritsos stuck on his exile island in the Aegean transforming roots and stones, artist Sergei Parajanov in prison pressing reliefs into aluminium bottle tops . . . working at all costs).

There's a tremendous dynamic here, not yet spoken of but inherent in these pages: the stirring tension between the single, singular picture (the record sleeve, the album's I.D., its passport shot, era-definer, conduit of pure intention / atmosphere, framing the scene – choose your favourite – lean it visible as you listen) and the total gallery leading to its primary selection. Think of the fabular calligrapher, producing thousands over years so that, when the emperor calls, they can deliver the 'one'. Here is a larger argument about the nature of the seen – how much do we, actually – in an age dominated and defined by the visual. Are the tumbling towers of 9/11 the last collectively received image on a global scale? SD understands saturation when the impact of the single is almost impossible now to achieve. And yet, select one must. So why not both approaches? You can have the pyramid's apex and the base, the sailing iceberg and its submarine vastness. Keep everything. Keep working. Wait.

Then look over and log the band at ground level, throwing ideas at Godrich like a new kind of frisbee that's not yet been invented; while TY, restless as a first thought, is up and down those stairs like he's on a cardio loop. Should we term these approaches 'strategies'? It feels far too conscious, especially early in the game. Were their methods unsound? It seems at times there wasn't any method at all. It sounded better backwards in another room . . .

Like Spinning Plates, the whole place was up for grabs, a closed circuit more open than the arms of lovers. Everything's being cut up. The band was playing to the gallery, literally. There was a growing sense that the space was becoming the work – and the reverse. Sounds rose like bread. SD was painting them, drawing them, scratching them into two dimensions – this is what the music looked like. It was a synesthete's convention: see hear for more. At the end of the day, there is no arrival, only a more or less successful handling of the goods. Sequencing was everything: texture. Perhaps these are the last albums – in the sense of an entirety – to matter as albums – words, sounds, images liberated, onward to the stars . . .

Subsequent –
Decreation (Carson, Anne)
A Room of One's Own (Woolf, Virginia)
Towers Open Fire (Balch, Anthony & Burroughs, William S.)

*here Was No * on *hom Yorke's *ypewri*er

*here is no al*erna*ive*

Meanwhile, on another machine in a different room . . .

When the Talking Heads album *Remain in Light* was released (8 October 1980) it offered a visual and conceptual relay baton forwards with its computer-generated back cover sleeve design – red warplanes flying in formation over the Himalayas, enigmatic but undeniably compelling. There was no knowing who would take this and run with it. We found out twenty years later (2 October 2000) when the peaks reappeared as if the flight was still under way. What had changed, however – or deepened – was the nature and extent of the assault, both climactic *and* state-sponsored, towards civilian populations. Red alerted us in ways we would not have imagined. Horror was *Brought to Light* and remained there.

akeway –
Regarding the Pain of Others (Sontag, Susan)
The Republics (Wahl, Huw)
The We of a Position (L.S., Lotte)

T
—
171

Universal Sigh

From 1580s: 'whole world, cosmos, totality of existing things', from Old French, from Latin, 'all things, everybody, all people, whole world', literally 'turned into one' and 'to turn, turn back, be turned; convert, transform, translate; be changed'; sigh, from Middle English, Old English: perhaps echoic of the sound of sighing

I realise this falls outside the scope of our assessment but, actually, it doesn't. There's a great pic from 2011 of SD swigging from a bottle (glass – important) of mineral water while TY has his photo taken with a young Muslim woman outside Rough Trade East. Off camera there is a very long queue. Everyone's there to pick up a copy of the newspaper produced alongside the release of *The King of Limbs*. On the *Evening Standard*-style paper-seller's booth a sign declares that 'All Can Become Normal Again'. There's a lot to unpick here, which we're not going to do now. And, at the time of writing (Spring 2021), it yet again feels somewhat ahead of the curve . . .

In Pedro Costa's film essay *Where Does Your Hidden Smile Lie?* Jean-Marie Straub says, 'A sigh can become a novel.'

Will the sigh be the last (mournful) music on earth? That is, until the next last time (spend even just a couple of hours with Ouspensky and this starts to seem extremely likely). The newspaper – as with the whole body of work – is presented as evidence of what we have done to ourselves and to everything we touch (a terrible more-than-Midas who, in trashing the green for the gold, turns all to shit).

We have to hope, while we still can, that in the unreal still lies the real, in the inhuman the human, that in the driftwood shack, stacked on higher ground as the waters rise, we'll still incant, sing the spells, seek to exorcise the black stain, search for a coherence in the gale.

Useful –
Living Time and the Integration of the Life (Nicoll, Maurice)
Poems from the Edge of Extinction (edited by McCabe, Chris)
The Possibility of Life's Survival on the Planet (Keiller, Patrick)

U
—
172

Voice

From Latin: voice, sound, utterance, cry, call, speech, sentence, language, word; Old English: ability in a singer, expression of feeling, invisible spirit or force that directs or suggests

Early on in the procedure – of this assembly, not their millennial moment – I noticed that in email and Zoom exchanges SD and TY's screen monikers changed, and even – so it appeared to me – *during* the course of a particular to and fro. I took this as a sign. It seemed churlish not to, as that is what signs call out for; but a sign towards *what*?

I Might Be Wrong but, as referenced elsewhere, the persona is not the person, and the person is more than one. 'Je est un autre'; Rimbaud knew. SD is not SD when he's washing up or on the school run. He might be Donald Twain or Michael Mortgage. TY might be Heywood Floyd, Winston Smith, (Doctor) Tchock/y and Zachariah Wildwood . . . whomever he wishes or we wish or need him to be (in French *je suis*: 'I am' and 'I follow' are the same). His voice also knows this feeling of things and selves being various. It even doubts sometimes that it is its own voice – it is *confirmed* in this hesitation, sometimes a shout, a cry from the heights, a howl from the depths, sometimes just a murmur in a bell jar.

The Ur-voices of the human – affection (song, loose lips stir hips), warning (song, anger is also an alarum) and grief (song, the wail of lament) – meet in his. The sound can translate as a Gregorian chant to the loss of belief – the voice's keening 'despite it all, still I am' – and if you can hear this or feel it in the ground on which you stand to hear it, you are too, in the roar of the stadium or the single hours of the lonely vigil, and that might be all we have and, possibly, enough – somewhere, at least, from where to start.

Vital –
Consent not to be a single being (Moten, Fred)
Darkness Spoken (Bachmann, Ingeborg)
Personae (Tait, Margaret)

V
―
173

War

From Old High German: confuse, perplex

Past tense Present tense Future tense is how it's looking currently. As ever, it's Knives Out time. You and Whose Army? Good question: For an informed opinion, the two-term President Eisenhower was well placed. Until he held that position, there was barely a civilian bone in his body, but plenty on the fronts he served, in both the First and Second World Wars, overseeing the invasions of North Africa, Sicily, France and Germany. From there it was a short step or three to Army Chief of Staff, first Supreme Commander of NATO and the White House.

In 1953, towards the end of his first year in office, he gave his famous 'Atoms for Peace' speech to the UN. Eight years later, in his closing address as outgoing President (17 January 1961) he said, '(The) conjunction of an immense military establishment and a large arms industry is new in the American experience . . . we must not fail to comprehend its grave implications. Our toil, resources and livelihood are all involved; so is the very structure of our society. In the councils of government, we must guard against the acquisition of unwarranted influence, whether sought or unsought, by the military–industrial complex. The potential for the disastrous rise of misplaced power exists, and will persist.

'We must never let the weight of this combination endanger our liberties or democratic processes. We should take nothing for granted. Only an alert and knowledgeable citizenry can compel the proper meshing of the huge industrial and military machinery of defense with our peaceful methods and goals so that security and liberty may prosper together.'

Good to see that all worked out well. But the aggression now is no longer only military, or even insurgent, terrorising, gang and domestic, personal. There is violence beneath, behind, inside the visible. It's in the air and every look, gesture and interaction has somehow to contend with its fact, its evidence. It's genetic; coursing through breast milk, whale blubber, coral reefs. It's Himalaya high and Mariana deep. It is how we relate to reality, explicit or not. What if this crane looming over yet another block of apartments was as lethal as a cluster bomb, or that bank transaction as fatal as a drone strike? Follow the money and it might well be. Mind, body and machine are triangulating the kill zone, and it is total, as you know, as Radiohead knows, from the shocking Boyle Family-style Bosnian slaughter fields on. Families haul across oceans of sand and try the desert of the sea. As this was being written Trinidad Tabora, aged ninety-three, was smuggled into Texas, crossing the Rio Grande at night with family members to escape endemic violent crime in Honduras (one of the enduring legacies of US incursions in the 1980s). She is a wheelchair user.

Should we not be eaten by the children we once were, for all that we have done? All the funny men have gone home.

Business as usual (your name here) . . .

Wake-up calls –
Money City Sick as Fuck (Boyer, Anne)
War (Le Clézio, J.M.G.)
War and War (Krasznahorkai, László)

W
—
175

X Marks the Spot

From the Greek and the Hieroglyph: serpent, cross; be multiple (as Jean-Paul Belmondo declared in Pierrot le Fou*); make your mark, Gen X*

Everything in its right place . . .

Xerox this –
*Always Coming Hom*e (Le Guin, Ursula K.)
Correspondences (Michaels, Anne)
Thinking Without a Banister (Arendt, Hannah)

Yes

From Old English, Proto-Germanic: so be it!

You sir, you madam! Yes, you; are you 'Optimistic' about the future? Are you? Well, are you? Music exists as evidence of coming through. It is, regardless of the sung concerns, a confirmation that witness has occurred. There is a suspension of the pain while the pain is sung. So it is with the image. We saw this; we made this with our seeing. These are the affirmative acts, constantly required and revived ways of managing the fact of being mortal. SD – whose vision is anything but standard definition – knows this. TY too: he calls out to the millions as he whispers to himself: test yourself, against yourself, against the demands of the crowd, against the pressure of the real as you feel it in the world.

Be properly civic. In early 2020, two libraries appeared online. The National Emergency Library and the Radiohead Public Library. Be generous in your press on common ground. And your sons and your daughters shall prophesy, and your young men shall see visions . . .

You know you want it –
Alienation and Freedom (Fanon, Frantz; edited by Khalfa, Jean & Young, Robert J.C.)
A Human Eye (Rich, Adrienne)
The Meaning of Freedom: And Other Difficult Dialogues (Davis, Angela Y.)

Y
<u> </u>
177

Zyzzyva

Genus of tropical American weevils found in palms

Given this has been driven by language, and in tribute to where so much of this story has taken place, we should leave the currently declared last word to (the) Oxford (English Dictionary). There's always more to learn, but don't worry, it's not a competition.

We could have ended with the dreamed ziggurat, but that looks like it's being covered and might well be under construction at the time of writing. Let's meet there. We'll be kings not only of limbs but also of infinite space. That sounds like the blueprint in a nutshell.

So let's put something on while we're waiting. How about 'Pyramid Song'? Is a ziggurat a pyramid? Uh, more or less, let's check it later. For now, just follow the bouncing ball:

All my lovers were there with me
All my past and futures
And we all went to heaven in a little rowboat

There was nothing to fear and nothing to doubt
There was nothing to fear and nothing to doubt
There was nothing to fear and nothing to doubt

Zestful –
Prisoner of Love (Genet, Jean)
Resistance (Lopez, Barry)
Tell Me How It Ends: An Essay in Forty Questions (Luiselli, Valeria)

After

the sea, the standing stones, the turning constellations . . .

You are in a room – it is very late or very early or both – in this way you have the run of the clock – each wall has a window – every compass point is open to you – there is floor wall to wall for now but the roofing is uncertain – beyond the room you hear the sound – it is growing and it is the sound of a growing sound – what a sound sounds like as it becomes one – it is a sound which makes pictures in your eyes and it is a sound that makes a space in which you can be something you are not without it – you very much want to be part of that sound but you are not sure from which place from which hour it is coming to you – so you wait – you stare intently at your hand – at the labyrinth of your fingerprints – you feel the path to the sound is within you and without at the same time – it is the same path but it looks different in each place – it is bright and dark threatening and exhilarating – so you wait – at the edge of the times and the turn of relations – while everything you know everything about your life and place everything inside your head and not is just about to change . . .

Gareth Evans is a writer, editor, film and event producer.
He is Adjunct Moving Image Curator at Whitechapel Gallery, London.
He hosts the London Review Bookshop series 'Screen at Home' and lives in London.

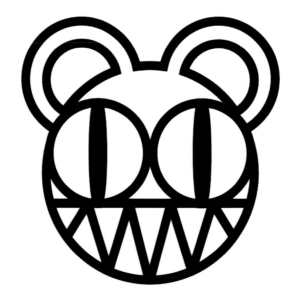

bear

this is not a tree

crunchedupcar

target 80s landscape cmyk

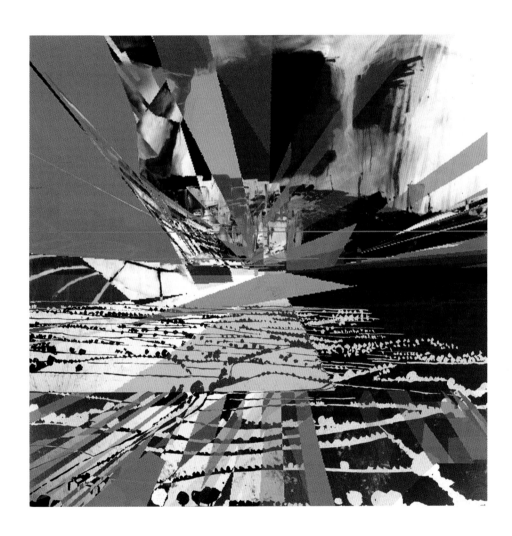

target 80s landscape

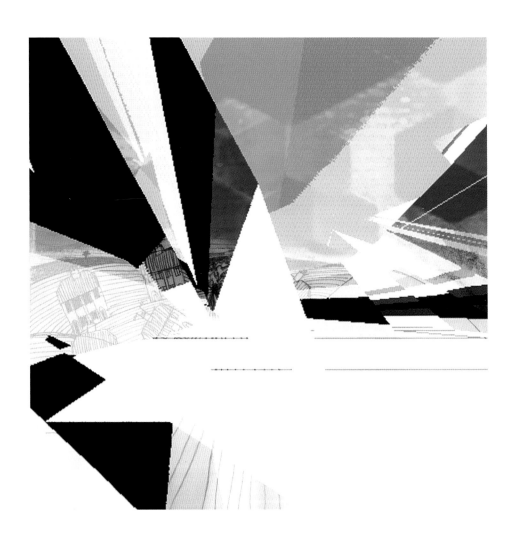

GMT land being invaded pointy

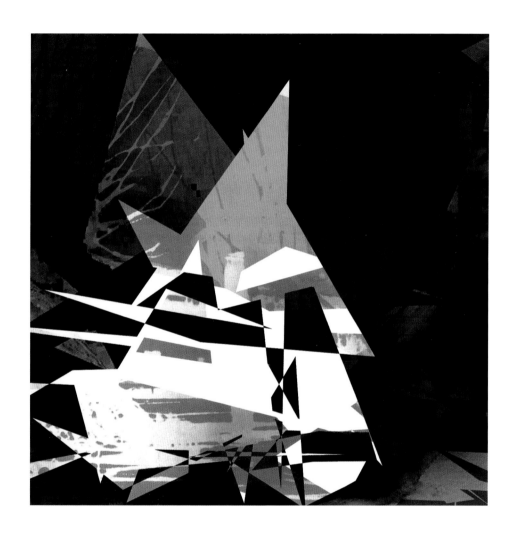

polygon fragbomb

GMT land being invaded pointy (detail)

wallpaper waterfall cymk

wallpaper waterfall

digi frag4

this feels like spinning plates

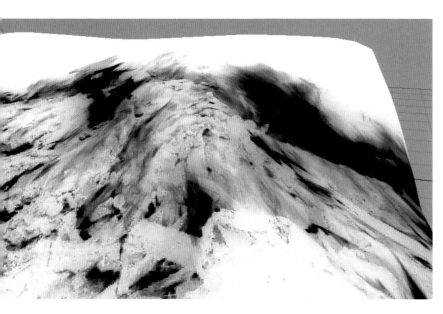

digi frag1 / millook ru6 / digi frag2

should have took the shot

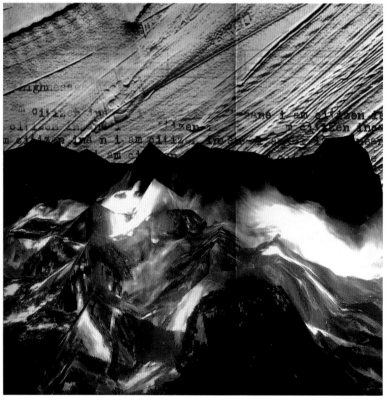

landing in the alps at night again / landing in the alps

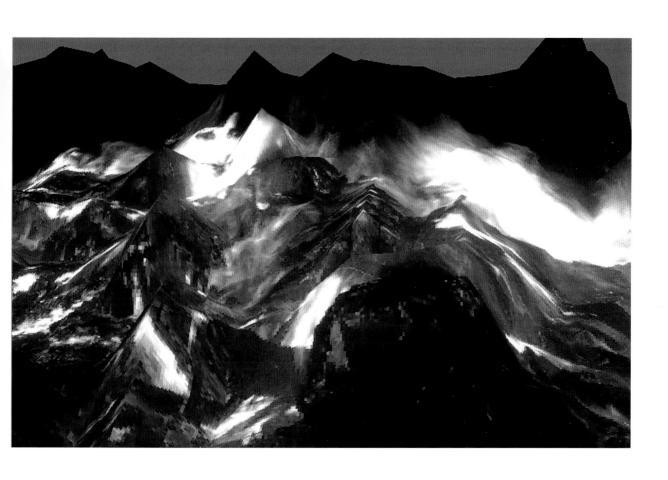

landing in the alps at night

fire 1 targa bw / fire 10 targa / fire 16 targa

fire 30

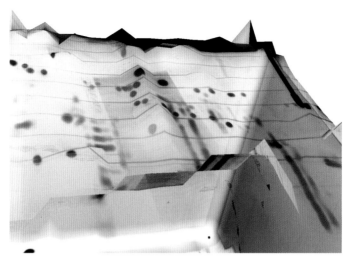

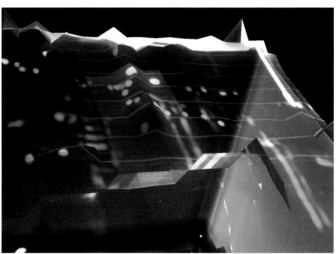

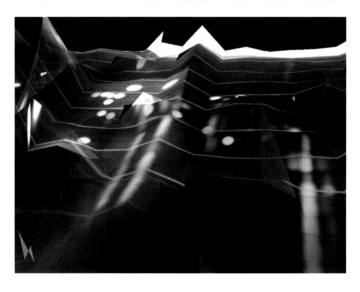

a star is / organ in 1st person / violet

sea rocks blah blah

electric violence

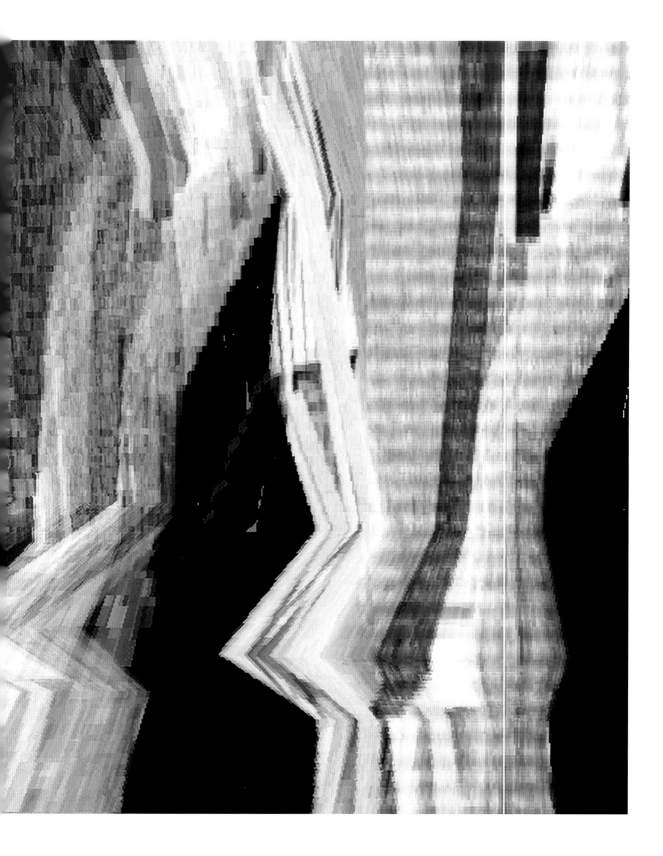

litewave / folded dam3

folded dam4 / folded dam6

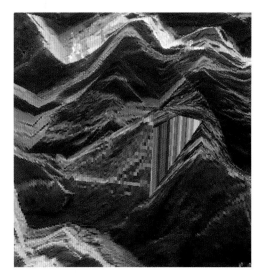

digifrag5 inv detail / digifrag5 inv detail2 / frag madness

digifrag5 / millook ru1 / millook ru3

pull yuself together

crunched up basement

crunchedupcar. the sequel2

fragment horizon targa

fragment horizon

volcanos bastardos silver2

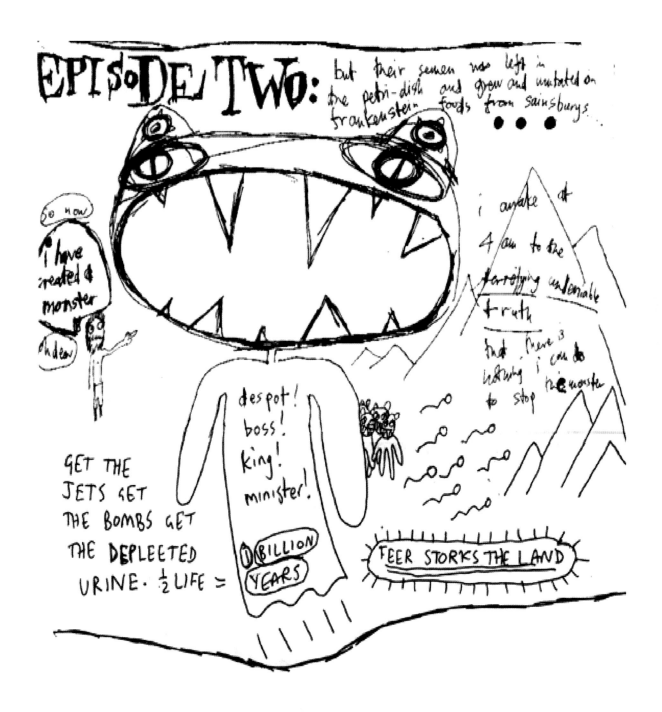

oh yeah / oh yeah 2

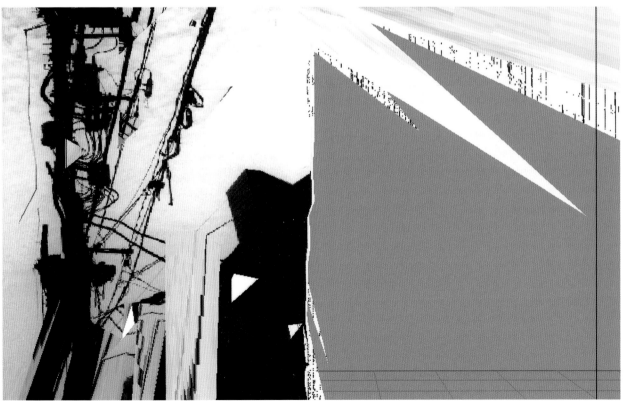

fizzy sticks (the final conflict)

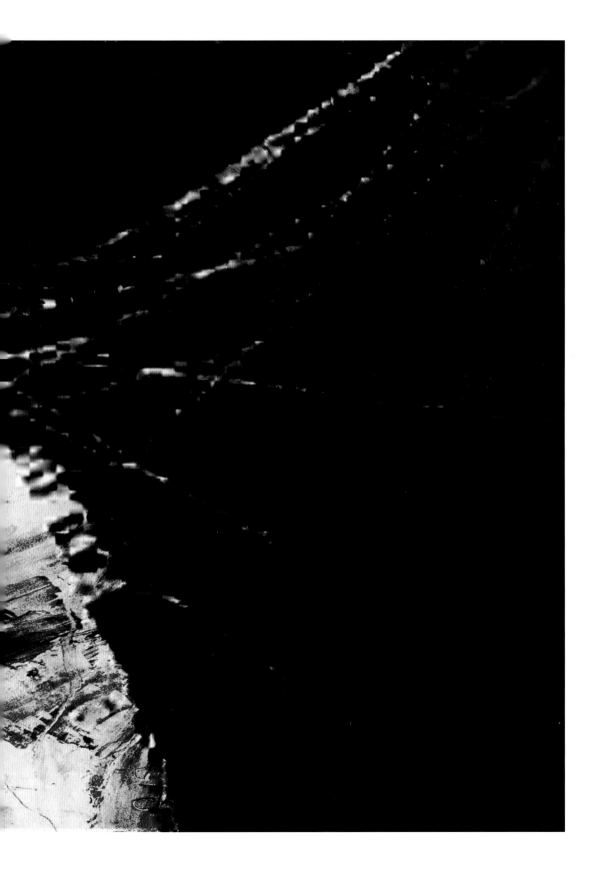

1st light painting / 2nd light painting

more ghosts, this time on tv

amateur poetry for yu:
cloud fucking cuckoo land.
for christmas i got yu
a still born prepacked newborn slave
to serve your every need
no blood no mess just reheat
ready to make your cushy numbered
mash potatoe comfort dayglo roadsafe trainers
so yor feet can take a rest from the struggle of the behest
responsibilities of power the terrible terrible strain
it must make on yor every waking hour on your playstation trigger finger on your disco dancing into
cloud fucking cuckoo land
into the wee small hours because we know how to have a good time in 1999
and lose some of that fat kidswatch the world collapse like a discontinued component in a newoutdatedappliance which

dear Rolling Stone
i thought
this might look
good in your
magazine
thom e yorke.

yu will soon throw on the scrap heap with the corpses and the fridges with the

cfcs+killerbees.

let s carry on marching into the light for we are gods chosen people 20 12 98.

amateur poetry   { 229 }

exciting new digital revolution

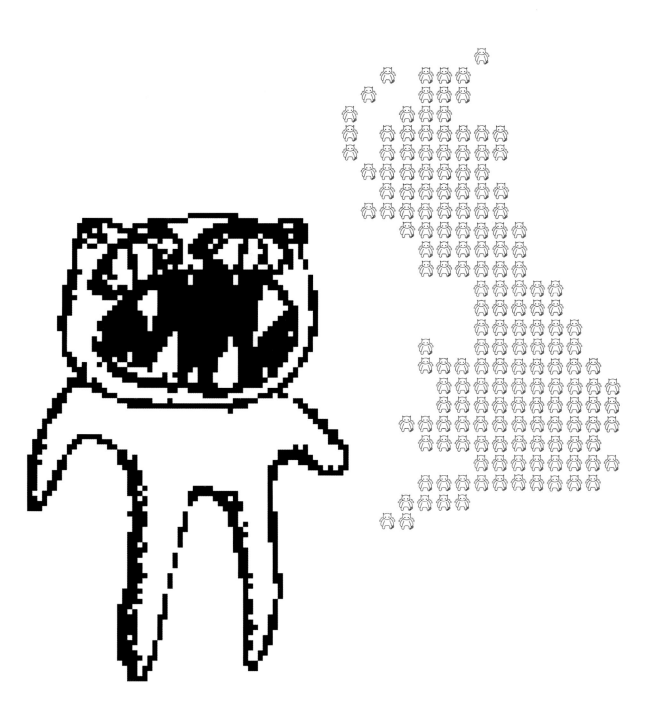

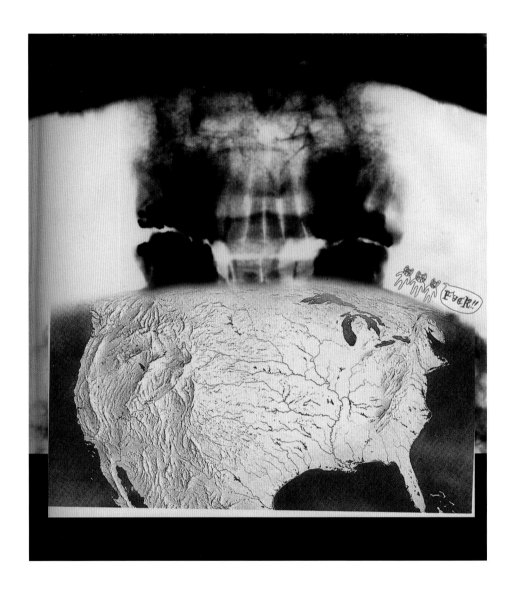

worldbomb teethfuck3

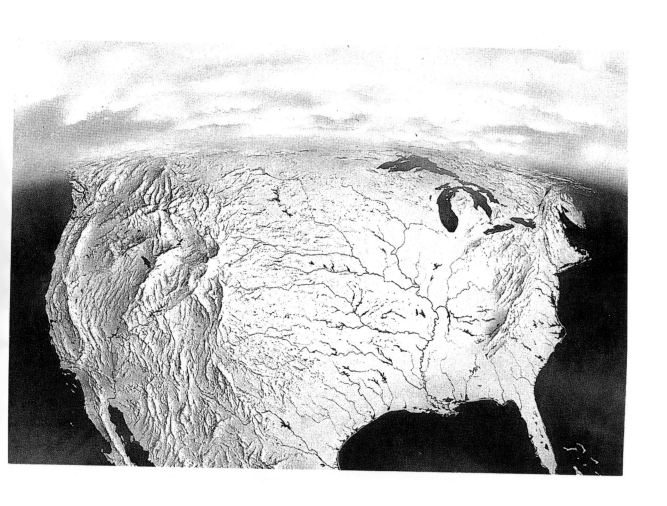

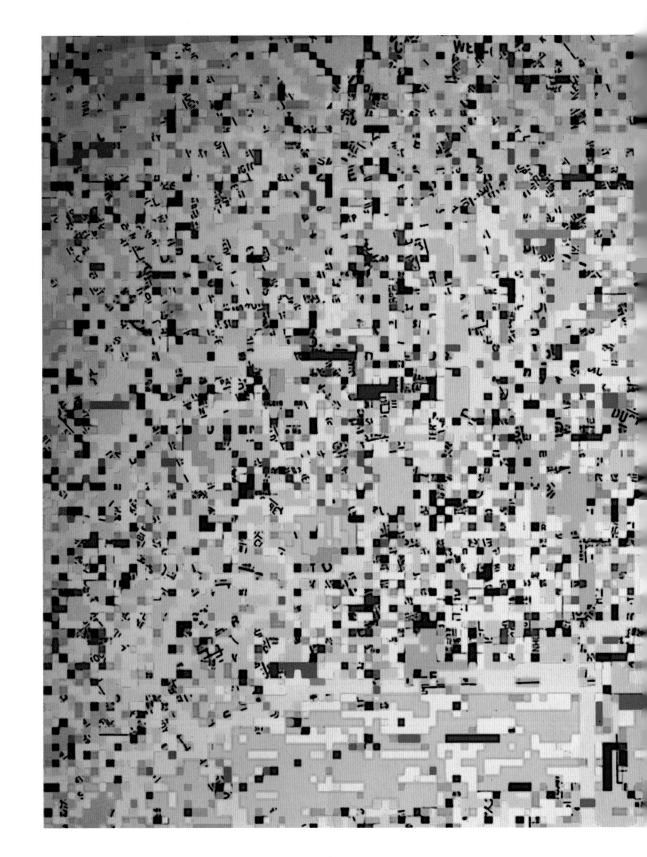

new troy

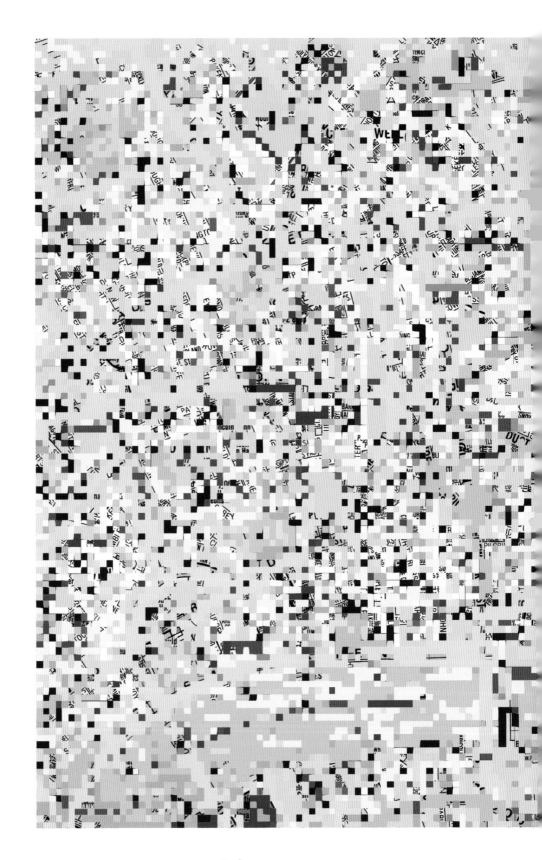

amazing!

jungle shots 1

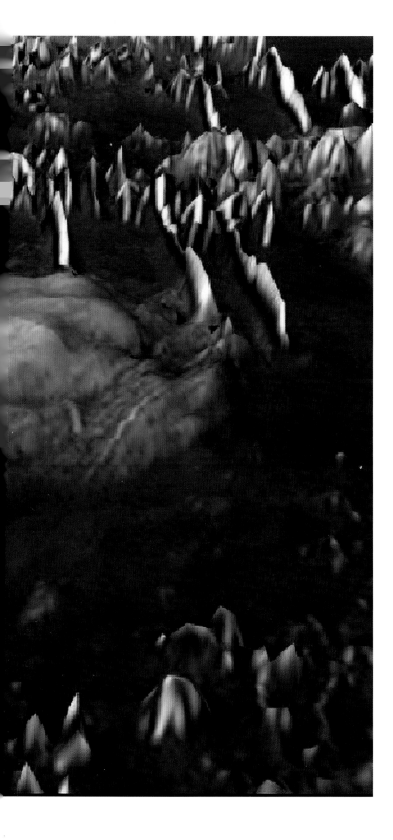

im lost at sea
don't bother me
im lost at sea
come round for tea
lie easily.
ive lost my way
come back to me
washed out to sea
come back to me
small comforts
red tape.
that s IT thats all there is
a fools goes on and on
motrbike on wall of death.
we all mistakes
and this is yours.
sooner or later youll have to learn.
lundi fastnet irish sea
i got a message i cant read
pharisle pharoah hebrides
i got a message i cant read
sucked inside out.
spinning plates trick
spinning plates im spinning plates
juggling knives
juggling knives
spinning plates
im juggling knives
i lowe you more than anyone else alive.
im on your side
nowhere to hide
im on your side
the most beautiful woman in the world
the most beautiful woman in the world.
im lost at sea
dont bother me
washed out to sea
come back to me
you are living in a fantasy world
im lost at sea
come back to me
trap doors i slide
and spiral down down down.
im on your side
hall of mirrors
nowhere to hide
i spiral down down down
you are living in a fantasy world
the sky is green
brain overload im so afraid
the trap door opens
i spiral down
down
down
down

bear lightscape

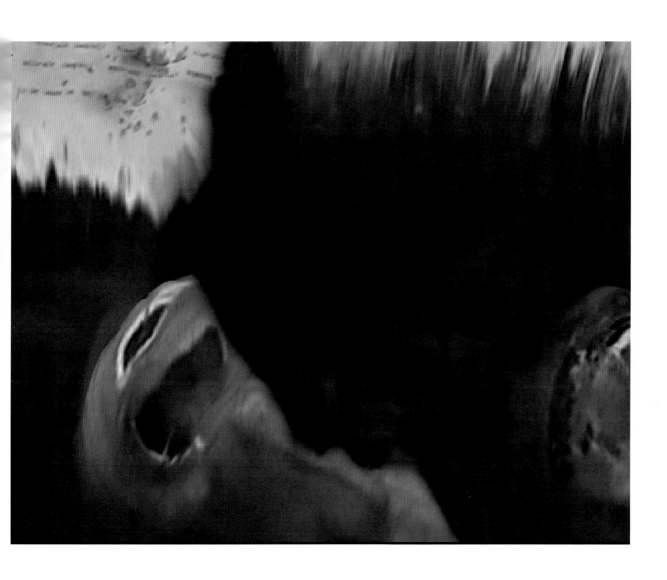

accidental shark lightscape

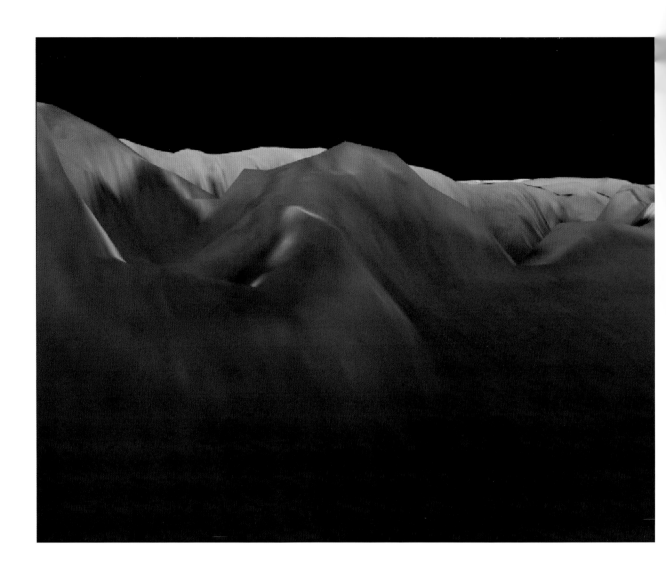

*lightscape *2*

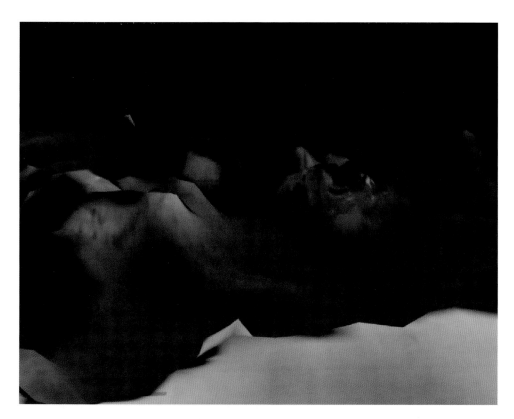

*lightscape *6 / lightscape *9*

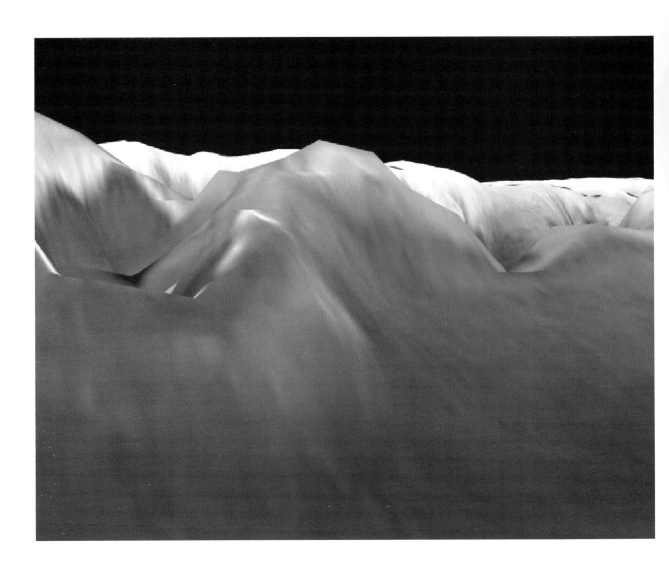

wave mountains ice

wave mountains ice crop dark

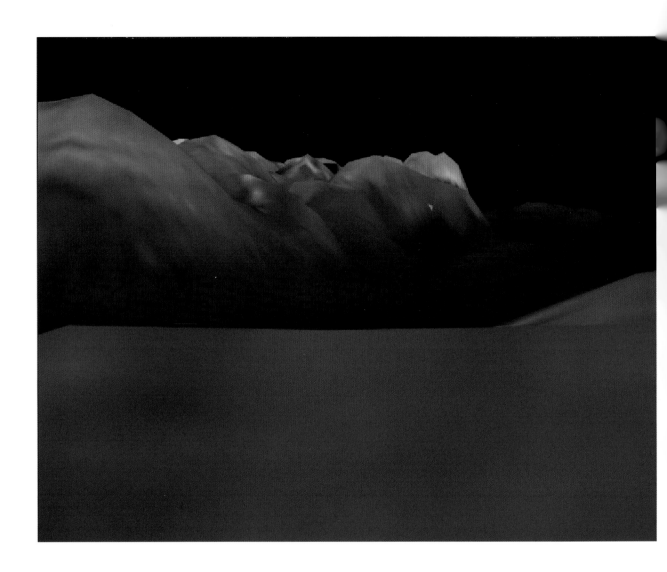

*lightscape *1*

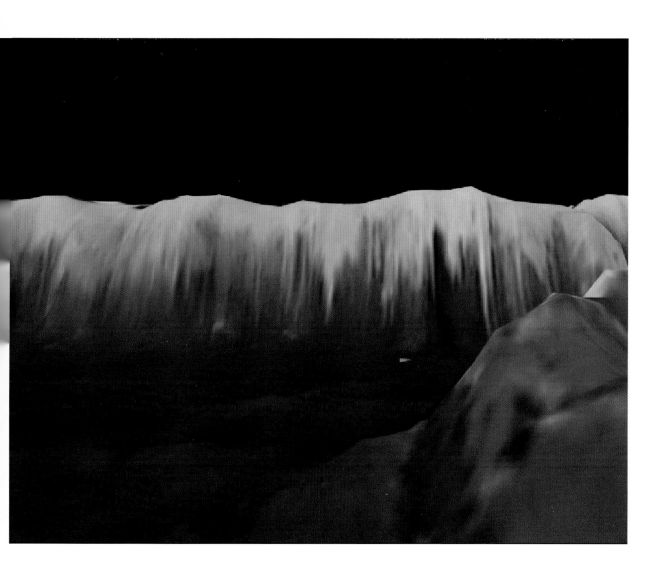

my second waterfall

lightscape *7

bug mound2

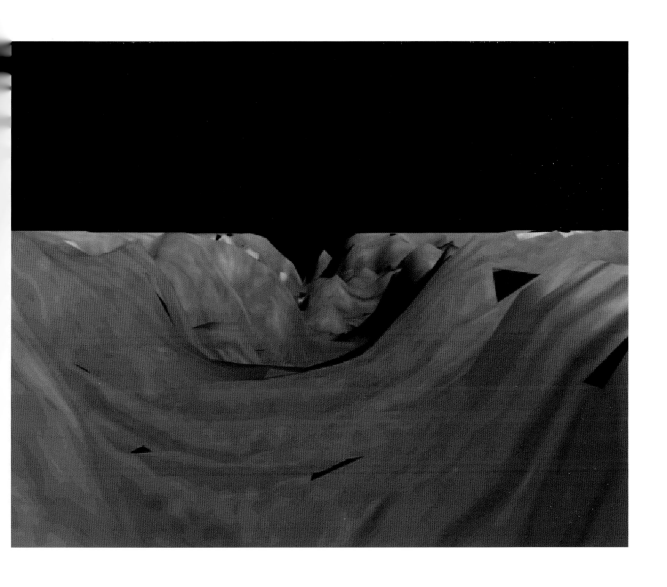

grand canyon

grand canyon 2

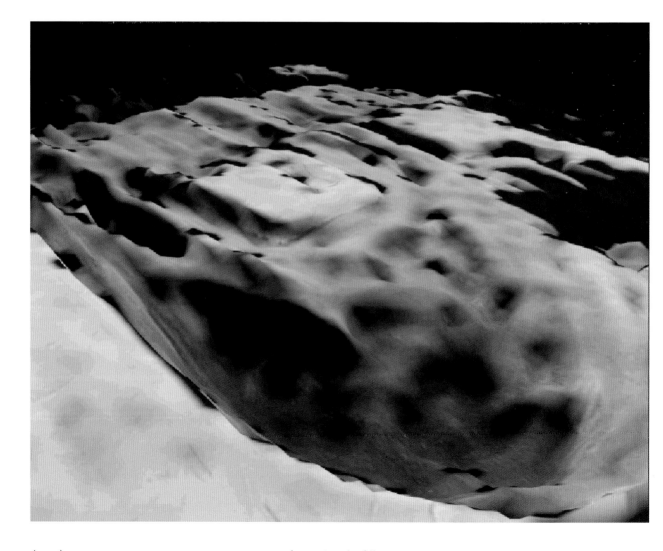

lumpy terraine biigg

recess cavatee2 detail

clicks on the phone

inexplicabel

unhinged

burn the heretics
burn the heretics
burn the heretics
burn the heretics
burn the heretics
burn the heretics
burn the heretics
burn the heretics

edges distort

inexplicabel

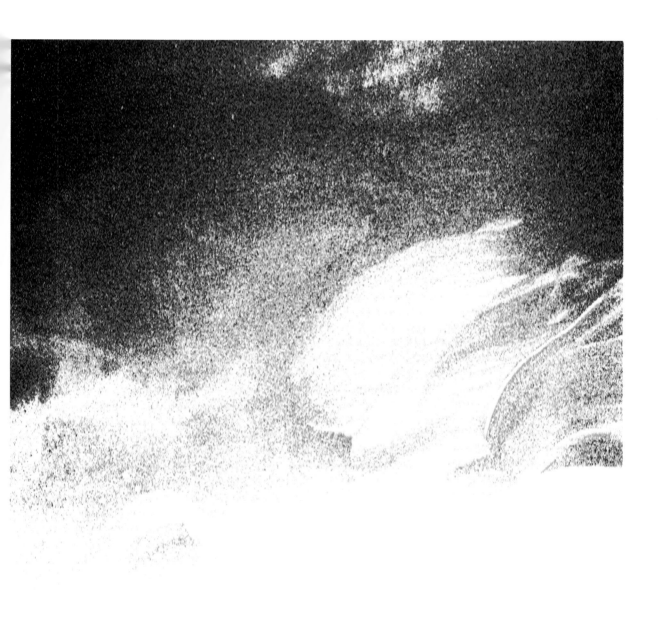

texture

clouds

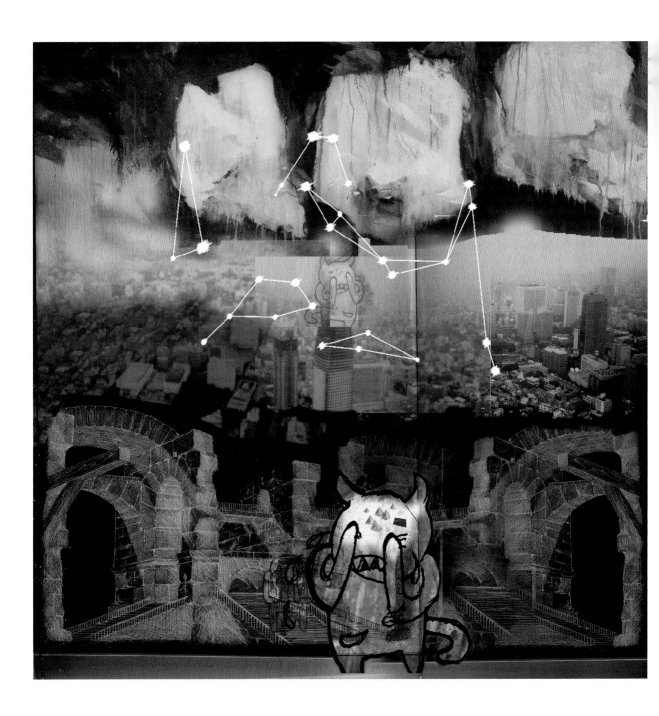

true city interior

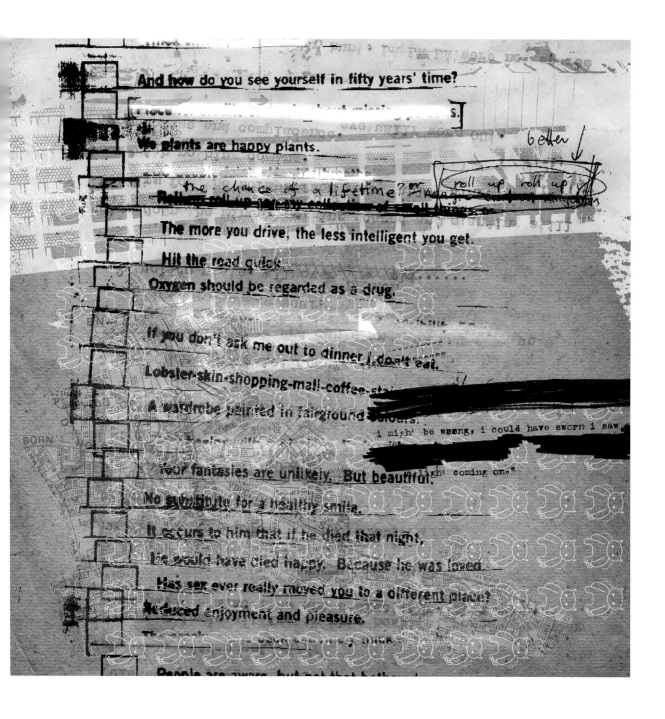

And how do you see yourself in fifty years' time?

s.

No plants are happy plants.

the chance of a lifetime? *better*

roll up, roll up

The more you drive, the less intelligent you get.

Hit the road quick.

Oxygen should be regarded as a drug.

If you don't ask me out to dinner I don't eat.

Lobster-skin-shopping-mall-coffee-sta

A wardrobe painted in fairground colours.

i migh' be wrong, i could have sworn i saw

Your fantasies are unlikely. But beautiful. *coming on."*

No substitute for a healthy smile.

It occurs to him that if he died that night,

he would have died happy. Because he was loved.

Has sex ever really moved you to a different place?

Reduced enjoyment and pleasure.

People are aware, but not that bother

true city interior (detail)

ice age coming

a conflict of interests   rubber bullets

middle england   people's princess

spin with a grin   well adjusted

no guilt/no conscience

windfall

trickle down compressor   weak reception

oh dear. how sad. never mind.

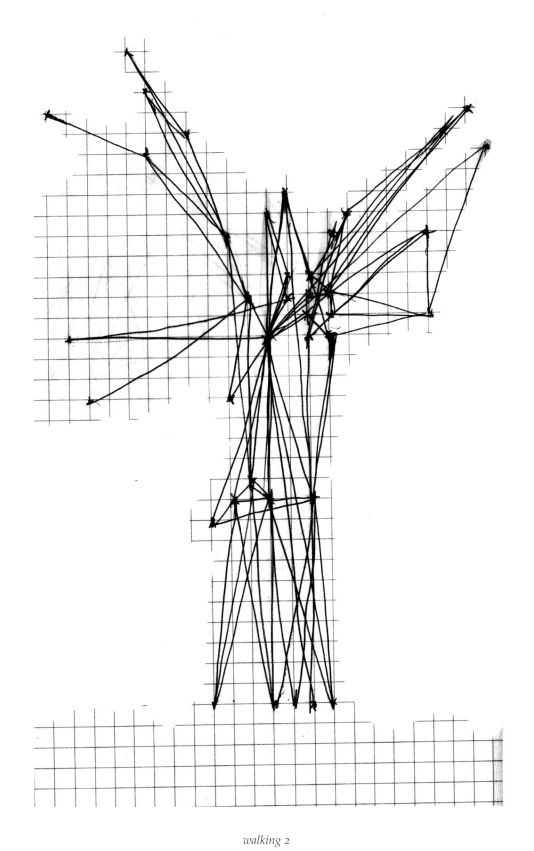

walking 2

ice age coming ice age coming

polar bear iceberg

glaciated landscape2

[copy/paste]Theres just the muffled crunchy sound of teeth grinding and scraping of boots on tarmac or something and a noise far away that maybe is someone crying or a cat and evrything moves a bit in the wind

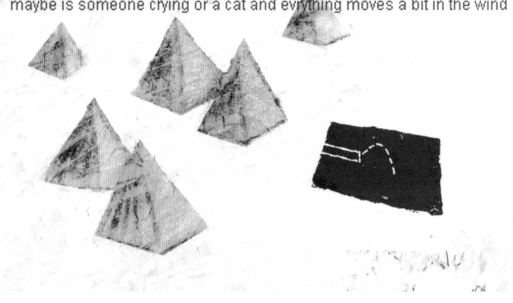

Evryone expects you to perform but you cant. Copy/paste but nothing happens. Undo but cant undo. Get text ha ha ha. Im a very busy person im sorry youll have to wait until tomorrow or maybe the next day if youre lucky. if im lucky. if im lucky ill still be here: hello how are you is evrything

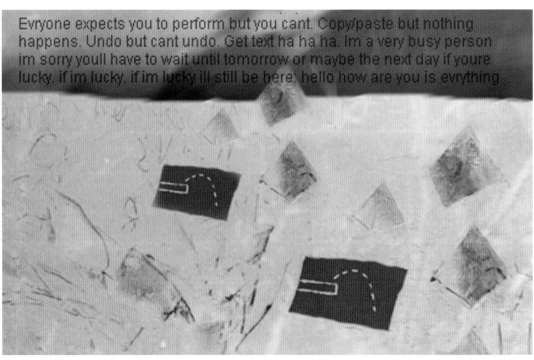

teeth grinding 3 / perform

red snow. bootprints. (details)

snow fields / hotels, fire, glacier 2

hotels and a glacier

target land

snow evidence but on fire 2

realistic flames

marsh drowning

ice drowning

world trade center (detail)

bears on air

your house = blue flash 2

demon / bears / blood cubes

your royal highnesses

    i am citizen insane i am citizen insane i am citizen isane
  i am citizen insane i am citizen isnsane i am citizen insane i
   i am citizen ins n i am citizen insane i am citizen insane i
 i am citizen insan i am citizen isnanse i am citizen insane i am
 i am citizen insane i am citizen insane i am citiz em insane i am
i am citizen insane i am citizen insane i am citizen insane i am citizen
 i am citizen insane i am citizen insane i am citizen insanni am
     BODIies floting
       walking ldregiane cranes. machine guns in hand.
          devils walking in jungles.

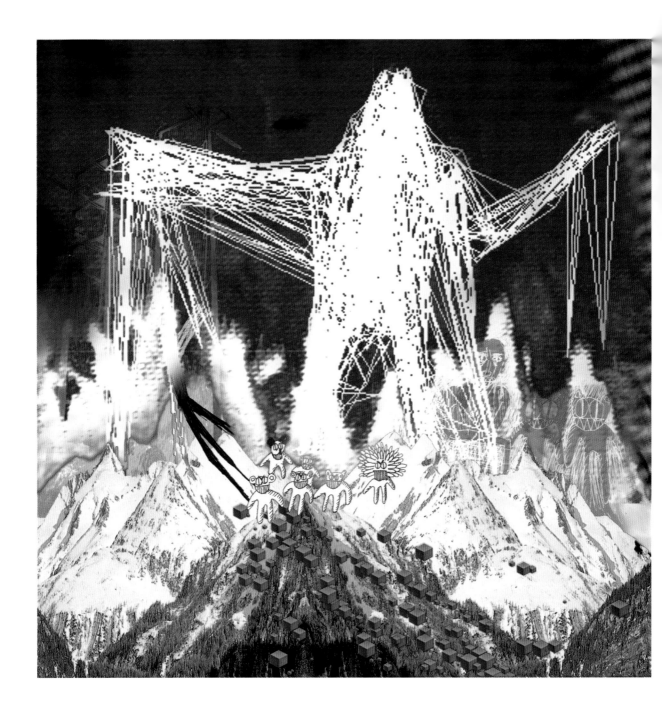

wire frame + austria3

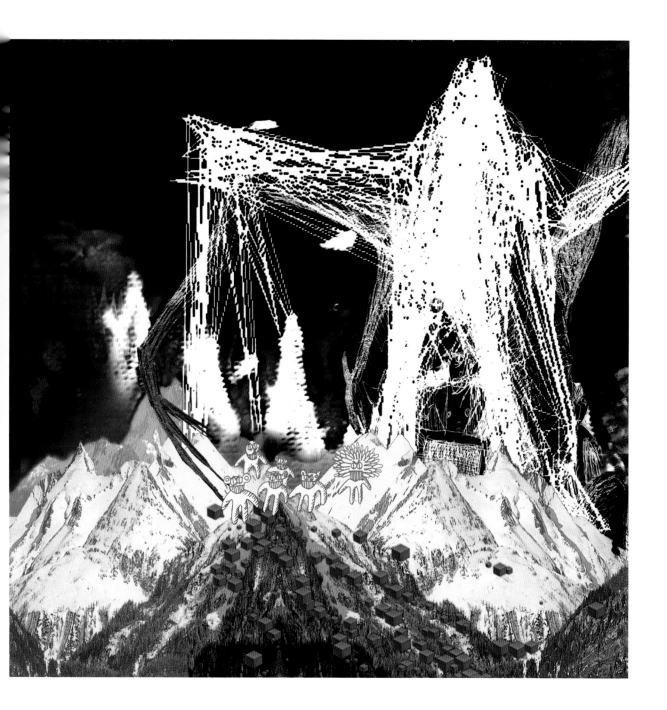

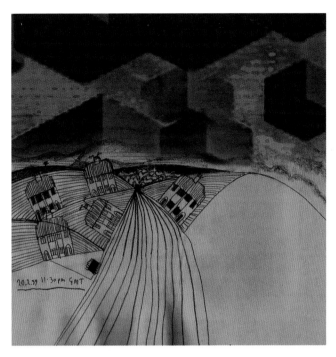

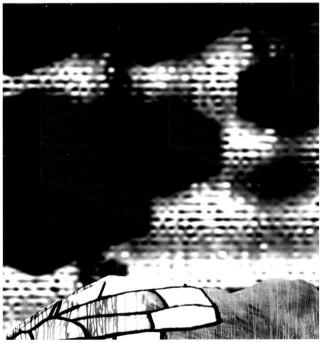

GMT land being invaded dark / bigblocks over cornwall

plunge to your fuckin doom you3

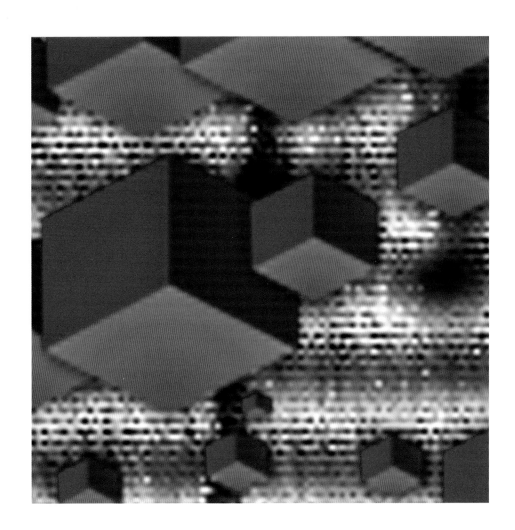

i crop zee bigblocks hardcore

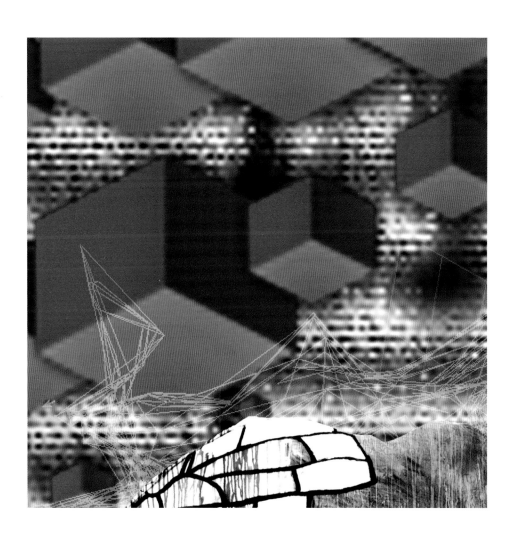

i crop zee bigblocks hardcore2

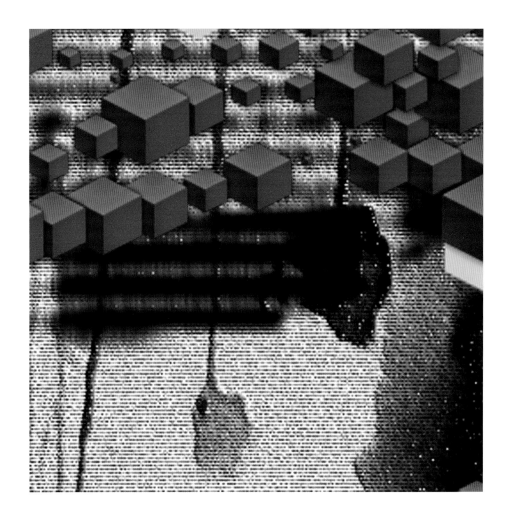

i crop zee bigblocks

My everyday life.

Thick smoke, no breeze.

And how do you see yourself in fifty years' time?

[Place for credits of movie about missing persons.]

We plants are happy plants.

200 people faint. Hard to breathe.

the chance of a lifetime? ~~Roll up roll up~~ *roll up, roll up* *better*

The more you drive, the less intelligent you get.

Hit the road quick.

Oxygen should be regarded as a drug.

Thick smoke not evenly distributed. Visibility 50m.

If you don't ask me out to dinner I don't eat.

Lobster-skin-shopping-mall-coffee-stained-lipsync.

A wardrobe painted in fairground colours.

Story begins with explosion. Ends with explosion.

Your fantasies are unlikely. But beautiful.

No substitute for a healthy smile.

It occurs to him that if he died that night,

He would have died happy. Because he was loved.

Has sex ever really moved you to a different place?

Reduced enjoyment and pleasure.

The smoke came back extremely thick and abrasive.

People are aware, but not that bothered.

Heavy artillery concealed in nose.

Everything I do/say is suspect.

A stranglers' hands.

One of us.

No autonomy. A lethal coctail. Horrific violence.

a lethal cocktail

devil in fire

volcanos bastardos twily / volcanos bastardos

volcanos bastardos darken

stalking toy2

the little lambs boundeth through the fields. they know the lord loves them. they know not from whence they came. they know not whither they go to. they hear not the approaches of the farmer with his 12 bore shot gun, who sadly must put a bullet through their re heads for nobody wants to eat them thanks to EEC directive 115. v.

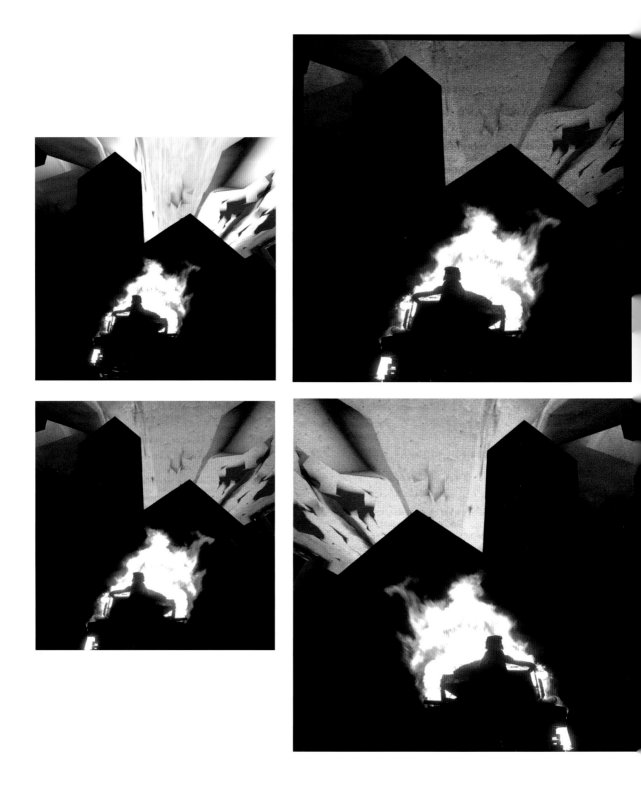

good as a film / burning city good version
grey city burning / 06 burning city

feed the chickens 2flat

astroboy

china dam

mm sexy bears

not such

NOTICE!

☞ TO THE PUBLIC!

RADIOHEAD

UNDER A BIG TOP
TRICKLEDOWN COMPRESSOR
UNSURPASSED NOVELTIES
GIANT COGS TURN
WELL ADJUSTED
THE ICE AGE IS COMING
RUBBER BULLETS
LAST REMAINING
POLAR BEARS

A GENUINE
FREAKSHOW
150,000 VOLTS OF ELECTRICITY!
MOBILES CHIRPING
CRACKS APPEARING BENEATH THE VENEER
ABBATOIR NOISES
WEAK RECEPTION
OUR NAME IS LEGION
CARROTS & STICKS

PACKT UP LIKE SARDINES IN A CRUSH TIN BOX

SHELLSHOCK, PARALYSIS, SLEEP-WALKING, any Child who is Backward in Study, and BAD HABITS of any kind PERMANENTLY REMOVED, Etc.

For a Due appreciation of the above INCOMPREHENSIBLE MUSICAL COMBINATION, much and a little more is depending on the Imagination of the Audience.

FEAR STALKS THE LAND!

I AM AWAKE AT 4AM TO THE TERRIFYING UNDENIABLE TRUTH THAT THERE IS NOTHING I CAN DO TO STOP THE MONSTER

POSTER BY STANLEY & TCHOCK

tent tour poster

COME ON KIDS

I SLIP AWAY
I SLIPPED ON A LITTLE WHITE LIE
WE'VE GOT HEADS ON STICKS
YOU'VE GOT VENTRILOQUISTS
STANDING IN THE SHADOWS AT THE END OF MY BED
THE RATS AND CHILDREN FOLLOW ME OUT OF TOWN
COME ON KIDS
THE BODIES FLOATING DOWNSTREAM
THE TRUCK LOADS WITH MACHETES
THE CAMERAS ARE TURNING OFF
YOU CAN WATCH
BIRDS PICK OVER THE BODIES
THE CAMERAS & THE FLIES
BLOATED JUST LIKE ROTTEN TREES
EYES POPPED OUT LIKE CIGARETTE MACHINES
THE MAKEUP WILL RUN
THE SET WILL ROLL AWAY
A SPIKE IN HIS FORKS
A CANE IN HIS SPOKES
YOU WILL SOON BE ON THE SCRAPHEAP IN BITS AND PIECES
I HAVE BORN A MONSTER
NO PULSE

STUCK ON FACE ▬▬▬▬▬▬▬▬
MY GUTS ARE WRENCHED AND CHEWED LIKE FLAT BALLOONS
SOMEONE HIT ME OVER THE HEAD
NOW I'M THE IMPOSTER

THE REAL ONE'S GONE FOREVER
BLOOD ALL OVER THE BATHROOM
TOO MUCH TO DRINK
I DIDN'T REALLY CUT IT
TOO MUCH OF A COWARD
TRUSSED UP IN TUXEDOS
WE'RE THE ORCHESTRA AT THE BALL
AND IT SLIDES LIKE SLIME
THROUGH YOUR WALLPAPER WALLS
WITH A GRIN LIKE ROADKILL
AND THE BLOODY POWER OF KINGS
I SNEEZE & IT'S AN EXOCET
I COUGH A NEW DISEASE

page from KID A hidden booklet

WE BOILED THE HEAD
WE DUG INTO THE MEAT
HE DID SOME OF HIS CARD TRICKS
FOR THE MAFIA GEEKS
I SAT IN THE CUPBOARD
AND WROTE IT DOWN
IN NEET

JUST AS AH SAW IT YEAH
JUST AS AH SAW IT
BUT IT GOT EDITED FUCKED UP
STRANGLED
BEATEN UP

THREATS HAVE DECIMATED
HOMES TO SLUDGE
CHILDREN SOON
AND SEALS
TURNING BEAR CIVILISATIONS
TO WARMING AND FLOATING
CREW DEAD
DAYS WILL FROM BOOM TO BUST
NORTH BIRDS PLEAD
FOR A HABITAT FROM VICTIMISATION
DROOLING
LOONEY
TUNES
MOVING IN SWARM
MOVING IN A SWARM
YOU HAVE SUCH AN AURA
DAHLING
CCTV IN EVERY ROOM
ZOOM LENS IN THE TREES
DON'T THROW STONES
YOUR ROYAL HIGHNESSES

page from KID A hidden booklet   {313}

HYMNS NUMBERED ON A BOARD
THE NAMES HAVE CHANGED
THE INNOCENTY
HAVE BEEN USED TO THICKEN
THE SOUPY
THE SOUPY CAN BE USED
TO FEED THE TROOPYS
FROM TIN CANS
HONEY FROM THE HONEY BEARS
NERVOUS MESSED UP
MARIONETTES
FOOD IS FOOD
&
SEX IS SEX
IVEHADMYFILL IWANTTODEFECT
TAKE THE MONEY AND THEN RUN
ONE PIXEL ON A SCREEN

GLAMOR.

WHEN YOR CHARITY SMILING
WHINING AND DINING
WE ARE BURIED BENEATH SIDEWALKS
THIS IS THE SOUND
OF BOOTS CRUSHING HANDS
STILL WEARING THOSE WEIRD UNIFORMS
IN THE END
IT WAS ONLY A GAME
GO BACK TO THE START AGAIN
& AS EVERY GOOD EDITOR KNOWS
WE ARE CABBAGE PATCH GIBBERING DOLLS
STRAW DOGS TO SCARE THE STRAWCROWS

page from KID A hidden booklet

RAW FISH DEEPFRIED MARSBAR
CONFIT OF MONKEY BRAINS
POT NOODLE
TURKEY BURGER
SOUTHERN STYLE
FINGER FOOD
BROKEN BRANCHES OF TWIGLESS TREES
I DINE ON ONLY
THE PREMIUM BRANDS
WATERFALLS OF MELTWATER
GENTLE NEEDLES
YOU CAN HARDLY FEEL
THESE WOODS AND HILLS
ARE THE TRADEMARK
OF WOODS AND HILLS
PLC
COUNTRYSIDE DEVELOPMENTS
GLACIATED AUTOINFERNO
LOVINGLY SCRAPING THE
BOTTOM OF THE OIL BARREL

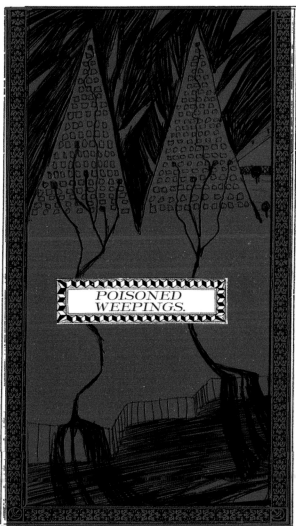

POISONED
WEEPINGS.

IN THE BUNKER
LIKE SITTING DUCKS
DO WE LOOK LIKE THE ENEMY TO YOU

500 POINTS
BONUS ROUND
HISTORY IS DYING
SORRY WE WERE ONLY KIDDING
HE'LL TAKE THE MONEY FROM UNDER YOUR NOSE
HE'LL TELL YOU ALL YOU WANT TO HEAR
HE PAINTS HIMSELF REFLECTIVE WHITE
TO REFLECT THE BLAST
WHEN IT COMES
HE WILL TAKE YOUR CHILDREN
AND HE'LL BREAK YOUR HOMES
HE WILL TELL YOU HOW HARD HE IS TRYING
BUT WE'RE ALL ON THE MARKET NOW
HE SAYS HE WANTS TO BE OUR FRIEND
HE SAYS HE'S ALWAYS BEEN ON OUR SIDE

TOUGH CHOICES
WITH DIFFICULT DECISIONS
THAT YOU REALLY
WOULDN'T
UNDERSTAND

page from KID A hidden booklet

FOR CHRISTMAS I GOT YOU
A PREPACKED
NEWBORN SLAVE
TO SERVE
YOUR EVERY NEED
NO BLOOD NO MESS
JUST REHEAT
READY TO MAKE YOUR
CUSHY NUMBERED
MASH POTATOE COMFORT DAYGLO
ROADSAFE TRAINERS
SO YOUR FEET CAN TAKE A REST
FROM THE STRUGGLE OF THE BEHEST
RESPONSIBILITIES OF POWER
THE TERRIBLE TERRIBLE STRAIN
IT MUST MAKE ON YOUR EVERY WAKING HOUR
ON YOUR PLAYSTATION
TRIGGER FINGER
ON YOUR DISCO DANCING
INTO CLOUD FUCKING CUCKOO LAND

INTO THE WEE SMALL HOURS
BECAUSE WE KNOW HOW TO HAVE
A GOOD TIME
AND LOSE SOME OF THAT FAT, KIDS
WATCH THE WORLD COLLAPSE
LIKE A DISCONTINUED COMPONENT
IN A NEW OUTDATED APPLIANCE
YOU WILL SOON BE THROWN ON THE SCRAPHEAP
WITH THE CORPSES
AND THE FRIDGES
WITH THE CFCS+KILLERBEES

AMOK

LET'S CARRY ON MARCHING INTO THE LIGHT

SO KNIVES OUT
CATCH DA MOUSE
SQUASH HIS HEAD
PUT HIM IN THE POT
THE MARCH OF THE KILLER ANTS
SIDEWAYS DOWN SIDEWALKS
CLAWS CLANGING
IN MELTDOWN-NOON-HEAT
FRENZY
LOBSTER-SKIN-SHOPPING-MALL
COFFEE-STAINED-LIPSYNCBODIES
ALL LICKETY SPIT

THIS IS YOUR
GOLDEN HANDSHAKE
THIS IS AN HALLUCINATION
AND THESE FACES
ARE IN A DREAM
A COMPUTER GENERATED ENVIRONMENT
A FANTASY ISLAND
YOU CAN DO ANYTHING
AND
NOT
HAVE TO FACE
THE CONSEQUENCES
YOU CAN PUT US
IN FREEZEFRAME
YOU CAN TOUCH WHOEVER
YOU WANT

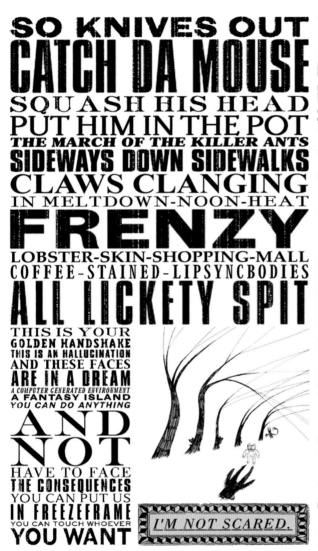

I'M NOT SCARED.

YOU CAN MOVE US
AROUND INTO COMPROMISING POSITIONS
STRIP US NAKED
SCREW WHOEVER ALTHOUGH
TECHNICALLY
WE WILL BE FROZEN TO THE TOUCH
SIT BACK DOWN AGAIN
AND PRESS
PLAY
LIKE NOTHING
HAS HAPPENED
PACKT LIKE SARDINES IN A CRUSH TIN BOX
PUPPETS ON STRINGS
INVISIBLE FORCES
SPEAKING IN A TONGUE
THAT DRIBBLES AND LASHES
SALIVATES IN THE ASHES
OF THE GAP IN BETWEEN
YOU & ME
BETWEEN YOU AND ME
THE GAP IN
IN BETWEEN YOU AND ME

I STAND AND WATCH
A TORNADO
ON THE FURTHEST HILLSIDE
KICKING ALL BELOW IT
INTO SOMETHING LIKE
THE WIZARD OF OZ
IT APPEARS TO WANT
TO STAY ON TOP
OF THE BLACK MOUNTAINS
SO WE ARE NOT CONCERNED
ABOUT IT
COMING
TOWARDS US

tornado poster

breaking house. hmoving speaking. old lord
sees noone for months. chaos,
    falling in love,
most weekends.
falling down drunk.

    lying in the gutter, passed out in the subway.
            back to work monday.
    back to work monday.
        hopeless case.
            howling down the ... chimney.
    release me. release me, please. o please. please.

don't be so pathetic. stand up. don't let yourself be run down.
    when game is lost,
    GAME OVER,
            space invaders. a broken heart.

            midas.

                shu||||||||

            the fuck up
    shut the fuck up
        shut the fuck up
    shut the fuck up

    Z((ZZZZ ZZZZZZZ ... ZZZZZZZ ...))

    buzy streets. construction. police corrup.

    ...ed crack, broken he... broken hearted.

    ...ing. endless whining. ... going on a bear hunt.
    ...we're not scared. terrifi... sh... show fear. walls have ...s.

            s...ini... ...les ...sk. subsi... be...ou a haleo...

shut the fuck up

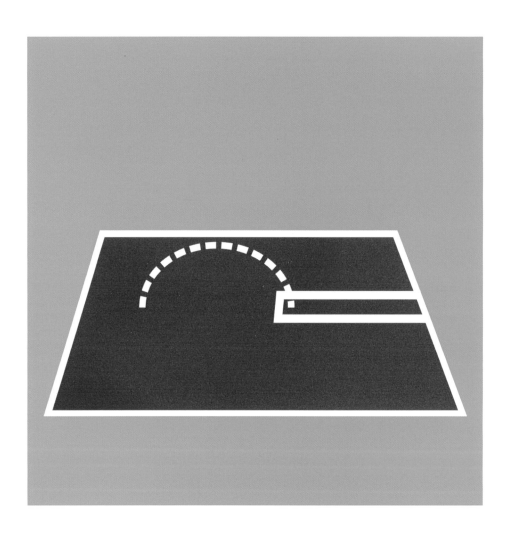

pool

rampant polar bear

children's bear2

Bear is going to work. What do you think Bear does?

bigger death bear

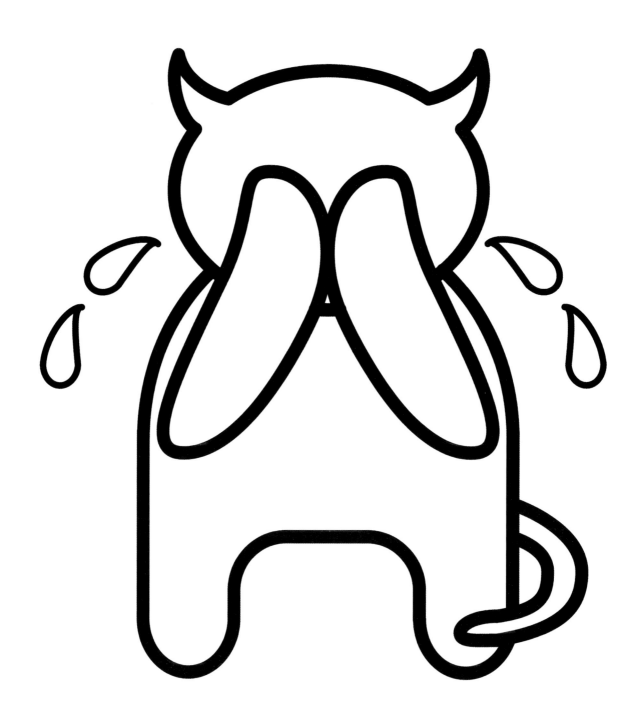

crying devil 3

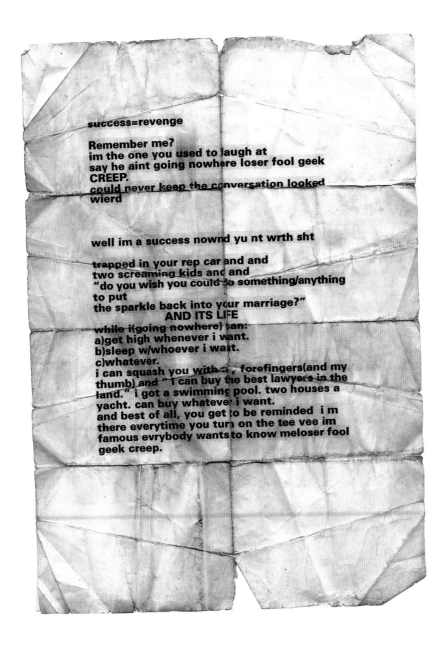

success=revenge

Remember me?
im the one you used to laugh at
say he aint going nowhere loser fool geek
CREEP.
could never keep the conversation looked
wierd

well im a success nownd yu nt wrth sht

trapped in your rep car and and
two screaming kids and and
"do you wish you could to something/anything
to put
the sparkle back into your marriage?"
                    AND ITS LIFE
while i(going nowhere) can:
a)get high whenever i want.
b)sleep w/whoever i want.
c)whatever.
i can squash you with a , forefingers(and my
thumb) and "i can buy the best lawyers in the
land." i got a swimming pool. two houses a
yacht. can buy whatever i want.
and best of all, you get to be reminded i m
there everytime you turn on the tee vee im
famous evrybody wants to know meloser fool
geek creep.

witness

this might be a cover

land of freedom™

THE DECLINE AND FALL OF THE
ROMAN EMPIRE

VOLUME II

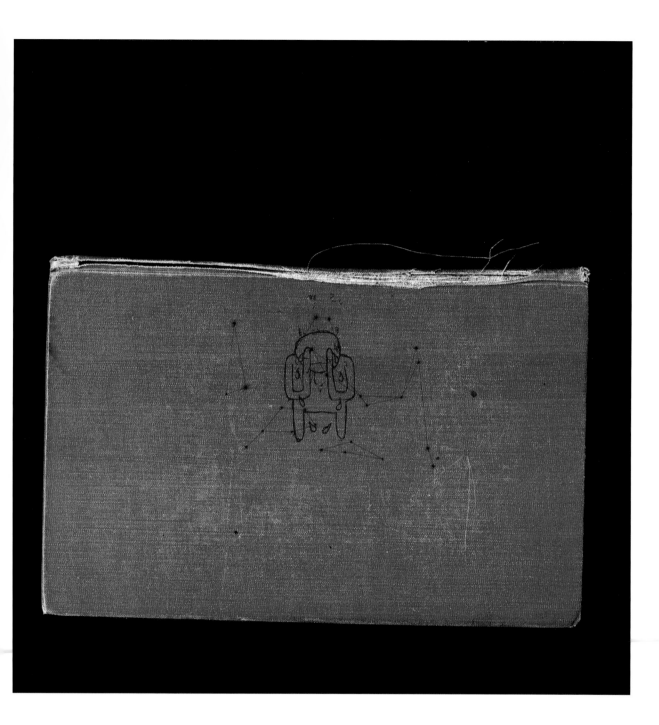

cover 2

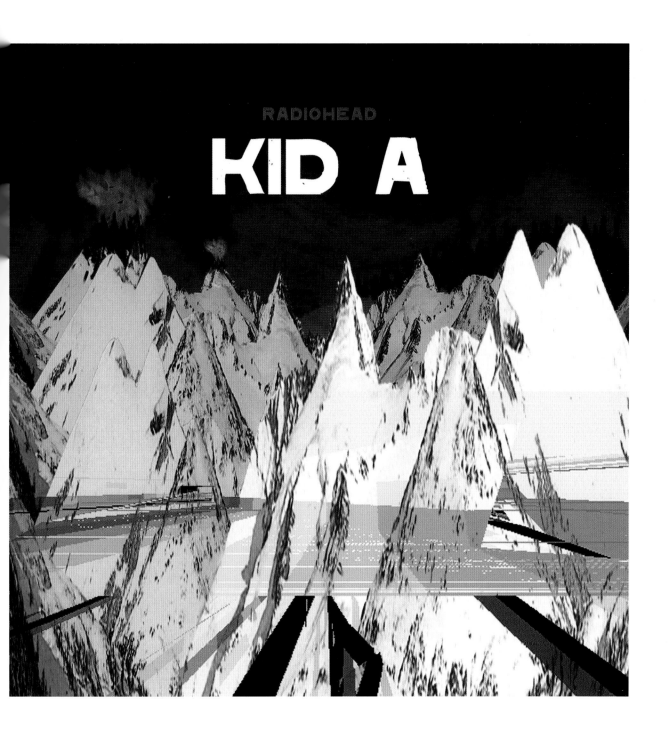

front cover